The Radical
SALES SHIFT

20 LESSONS from **20 LEADERS**
on How to Use Marketing to Grow Sales
in B2B Companies

LISA SHEPHERD

Note for Librarians: A cataloguing record for this book is available from Library and Archives Canada at www.collectionscanada.ca/amicus/index-e.html

ISBN – 978-1-77084-548-0

Printed in Canada ♻ on recycled paper

 FIRST CHOICE BOOKS

firstchoicebooks.ca
Victoria, BC

10 9 8 7 6 5 4 3 2 1

TABLE OF
CONTENTS

PART FOUR

20 LESSONS FROM 20 LEADERS   89

PART FIVE

Introduction

WE CAN'T FIND
ENOUGH HUNTERS

"We can't find enough hunters."

About twelve months ago I met Peter Saunders, who runs an industrial company called Clintek outside of Toronto that does $15 million a year in sales. Peter started ClinTek twenty years ago after leaving an account executive role at a multinational company. He had decided it was time to pursue his dream of running his own business, and ClinTek was born.

ClinTek has done very well over the years. Peter grew the company by leveraging his relationships in the industry and constantly innovating the services and products that ClinTek offers. In many ways, the company is a textbook entrepreneurial success story. The business employs forty-five people, is profitable, and serves a customer base of hundreds of companies across North America.

But lately, something has started to go wrong. The day I talked to Peter, he'd just fired another salesperson. That made three out of four he'd hired in the last two years. This latest salesperson had been with him for almost a year, and yet had

almost no sales to show for it, and
certainly none of the strategic deals
that Peter had hired him to pursue.

"We can't find enough hunters."

"We can't find enough hunters," Peter lamented when he and I met. "I need to find sales reps who will go out and hunt the kinds of customers that ClinTek needs – customers who will pay a premium for what we offer. We aren't a low-cost producer, so we don't compete on price. We have high-quality products and great service, which saves our customers money overall and solves specific problems they have. But those customers are hard to find so I need sales professionals who will go out there, find potential customers, educate them on what we offer and why it's valuable, and then sign deals. That's how we built up the company in the first place. I don't know how else we're going to grow the business." Peter sounded exasperated.

I commiserated and shared that I had heard similar comments from leaders of small and mid-sized B2B companies (ten – five hundred employees) with increasing frequency over the last few years.

What I didn't realize at the time was that Peter's remark would ultimately lead to this book. While Peter may have felt like he was dealing with an issue of salesperson incompetence, that wasn't what his real problem was – not by a long shot. What's going on is much bigger than one salesperson (or a few) at one company.

The World of Selling and Buying has Changed

In the last decade, something has changed in the business world – something radical.

It has to do with how people buy things – both when they're buying on their own behalf (as consumers) and when they're acting on behalf of the companies they work for in a Business-to-Business (B2B) context.

Think back to when you made a significant purchase around 2008. How did you buy a car, vacation, or business service? Chances are you did a bit of re-

search and then you talked to sales people —
be it in a dealership, at a travel company, or at
a business supplier. You probably had several
conversations with salespeople from different vendors before you decided what you
were going to buy, and then you started a ne-
gotiation process with one or two vendors to
get to a deal.

*Today, that's changed. Now buyers don't talk to
salespeople until much later in their purchasing process.
In fact, they wait to involve salespeople until as late as
they possibly can.*

B2B companies sell their products and services to other *companies* rather than to *consumers*. For example, manufacturers of engine components and professional services firms are typically B2B, while restaurants and movie theatres are B2C, business-to-consumer.

There's a growing body of research that reveals just how much the buying process has changed. Google ran an extensive study of the purchasing habits of
5,000 buyers. Among the findings, 71% of business people use the Internet on
a *daily* basis for their business purchase decisions.[1] I'll discuss this study in
greater detail in Chapter Two.

Buying behavior
has changed radically
over the last decade.

The Corporate Executive Board (CEB), a
member advisory council with over 16,000
members, has completed a study on the
change in B2B buyer behavior. Based on
a survey of 1,400 B2B buyers, CEB deter-
mined that on average, buyers complete 57% of their purchase process before
they engage salespeople from potential vendors.[2] Even with the complexity of
some B2B sectors, no one in the CEB study had completed less than 45% of
their purchase process before they contacted a salesperson.

1   http://bit.ly/1qjVlBy

2   http://bit.ly/Z53wx2

57%
COMPLETE

| START OF BUYING PROCESS | CUSTOMER'S FIRST CONTACT WITH SUPPLIER | END OF BUYING PROCESS |

The research firm Forrester has even more startling data: buyers are anywhere from 67% to 90% through their purchasing journey before they contact vendors.[3]

These studies show how much traditional salespeople are left out of the purchasing process. Because buyers can get so much information online, they can control much more of the buying process themselves – and they do. This often eliminates the opportunity for salespeople to get involved in shaping a buyer's decision. It doesn't change the importance of salespeople in closing deals, but it impacts how many deals those salespeople get the opportunity to close.

What the Change Means for B2B Companies

For B2B companies, the implications of the new buying process are far-reaching. There's a new reality when it comes to revenue generation: marketing matters.

For decades, the sales department has been the driver of revenue for B2B companies. When I started working in the early '90s for a computer equipment company, there were ten salespeople and not a single marketer. The company's revenues were about $20 million. Marketing, other than preparing sales support materials and coordinating the company's presence at trade shows, was not necessary. It was the salespeople who brought in the deals, from start to finish.

---

3   http://bit.ly/1tUNKQs

Today that kind of reliance on a sales force only, with no strategic marketing, is causing a lot of good B2B companies to struggle.

It's Time to Reinvent the Revenue Engine

Many strong B2B companies are now struggling to achieve their revenue targets. They tend to be companies who are exceptionally good at operations and whatever it is they do – manufacturing, fabricating, servicing, designing, evaluating, or some other product or service. They're also good at selling – that's why they've been successful in the past. But today's mode of sales, with the buyer in control, is a new frontier for B2B companies. The revenue generation leaders of these companies dream of finding hunters who will work their rolodexes (or create rolodexes) and bring in new customers and deals. Just like Peter Saunders at Clintek.

Today's mode of sales, with the buyer in control, is a new frontier for B2B companies.

But even if they were to find an exceptional salesperson, revenue would be unlikely to materially and consistently grow. Why? Because buyers have changed. They no longer answer their phones, return unsolicited phone calls or emails, attend trade shows, or sit through sales presentations for products or services they don't urgently need.

Marketing gets companies found when a prospect is looking for solutions. Marketing nurtures leads until they're ready to talk with a salesperson. Marketing makes sure the sales team has effective tools to convert prospects to customers.

With the buyer in control and completing 45% – 90% of the purchase process before they engage with salespeople, companies need to find new ways to engage potential buyers early in their purchasing journey. Or better yet, to initiate the buyer's journey. Since buyers don't want to engage with salespeople until they are more than halfway through making a decision, companies need to think of ways outside the sales department to engage with prospects who might need their goods and services.

For most B2B companies, that means marketing. Marketing is the function that raises awareness in the market, educates buyers on a company's solutions and expertise, and builds credibility. It's marketing that can help a company be found and contacted when a prospect is looking for solutions, nurture leads until they're ready to engage with a salesperson, and ensure the sales team has the tools and materials needed to support prospects in their purchase decisions.

Marketing is now the key to the first half of the revenue generation cycle. It's the door to opportunities with new customers and selling at a more strategic level.

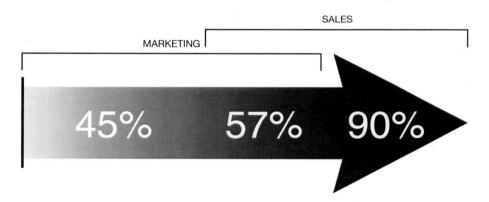

The challenge for many B2B companies is that marketing has never been a business function that's been needed in the past. As with Peter Saunders, marketing isn't even something that comes to mind when a B2B company leader is thinking about effective ways to drive sales.

Marketing is now *the key* to the first half of the buying process. Without it, B2B companies don't get the opportunity to sell.

Who Should Read *The Radical Sales Shift*

The Radical Sales Shift is for anyone who's in charge of revenue generation. Your title might be CEO; President; General Manager; VP, Sales; VP, Sales and Marketing; or something else. If you're responsible for revenue generation and find your company struggling to meet revenue goals despite significant time and investment in the sales department, this book is for you.

The Radical Sales Shift is especially for leaders of small and mid-sized B2B companies who have not used strategic marketing in the past. This book will provide you with the tools to reshape how you generate revenue – by focusing <u>outside</u> the sales department.

The goal of this book is to provide you with a better understanding of how to succeed in marketing. Too many businesses don't understand what's required to make marketing effective, and they end up walking away from their marketing efforts believing that it doesn't work for their business. But most companies who fail in their attempts at marketing do so because of a failure of execution, rather than a failure of the function. Marketing is all about how you use it.

How to Use *The Radical Sales Shift*

This book has five parts that you can read cover to cover, or you can choose chapters based on your needs.

PART ONE provides context and background – the data and insight on the shift in buyer behavior and what it means for B2B companies. If you are putting a business case together for your company on how marketing is now essential to B2B revenue generation, you'll find the data you need to make your case in this section. And if you're looking to confirm your perceptions about how the world of buying and selling is changing, this is where you'll find how the New Buyer looks and acts so you can structure your revenue generation activities appropriately.

PART TWO outlines what the New Buyer means for how B2B companies generate revenues. It presents three areas where changes in how companies use sales and marketing are yielding impressive results; the new funnel, sales team structure and resources, and the new role of marketing.

PART THREE includes three diagnostic tools. Some companies experience revenue generation difficulties because they need to launch, recalibrate, or enhance their marketing. Others have a weak sales staff or their sales and marketing teams aren't working well together. The diagnostics will help identify where the problems are and how to improve the revenue generation machine.

PART FOUR is a road map for revenue generation – the twenty lessons. Based on interviews with B2B revenue generation leaders, I've identified critical ways that great companies are making the transition from being sales-dominant to balancing sales with strong marketing, and are increasing their revenues and profits as a result.

And finally in **PART FIVE**, there are a few last words of guidance. Many companies who try to make marketing work will stumble. In this last section I share the "Seven Deadly Sins of Marketing" as a reminder of what it takes to succeed.

With Revolution Comes Opportunity

Traditional B2B companies have an amazing opportunity in the next decade. They have the ability to put marketing to work for their businesses. Marketing helps B2B companies accomplish important goals including:

- raising awareness of their products and services
- enhancing the profile of their company in the market
- attracting new customers
- achieving price premiums and getting sole sourced
- retaining and growing profitable customers
- growing their revenues and profits

In this new era in which the buyer (whom I call the New Buyer) is in control, marketing is becoming a competitive advantage and a fundamental function for B2B companies. If you're responsible for revenue generation in your company and are thinking that marketing can form an important part of how your company generates revenue in the future, you're right. This book will show you how.

> *Marketing* is now a competitive advantage for B2B companies. Are you putting it to work in your business?

Get in Touch

Things are changing fast in B2B revenue generation. New tools and techniques launch every year. I'd like to hear your questions and experiences. Please drop me a note at:

Email: lisa@theradicalsalesshift.com

Twitter: @MezzLisa

Blog: http://themezzaninegroup.com/blog/

The Mezzanine Group: www.themezzaninegroup.com

And for anyone looking to reach Peter Saunders at ClinTek, you'll find he's difficult to locate. That's because Peter is both real and a composite — he represents about a dozen CEOs I met over the last year who shared a similar experience. Rather than single any one of them out, I created an amalgam who represents their combined experiences and outlook.

PART ONE

BACKGROUND

This section provides data and background on the shift in buyer behavior and what it means for B2B companies. If you're building the case for marketing in your company, you'll find useful facts here to help support your argument.

CHAPTER *One*

A Brief History of Sales

It can seem that the sales department is the only way to generate revenues. It's been the mainstay of revenue generation for decades, so it's hard to imagine any other way for companies to generate sales. But in fact, it wasn't always this way.

In the early days of business, merchants sold goods to local customers directly. There weren't *any* salespeople because they weren't necessary – the merchant could handle both the production and the selling of the goods.

The Industrial Revolution changed everything. Suddenly, manufacturers could produce massive quantities, more than was possible for any individual to sell locally. So to maximize revenue, companies needed to find customers farther afield. And suddenly, sales became a specialized occupation.

In the United States the profession of sales exploded with the advent of the assembly line – the number of salespeople grew from just 600 in the year 1900 to over 2 million by the 1920s.[4] At first, salesmen (and they were sales <u>men</u>) were independent. They travelled on their own, created their own schedules and routes, and developed their own techniques. But that evolved over a few decades - as management systems at manufacturing

---

4   Abstract of the 15th Census of the United States 1930 qtd. in Powers, Koehler, & Martin, 1988).

companies evolved, the sales organization became more structured along-side the production lines. Salesmen started to be assigned specific territories and quotas, and followed the procedures and processes that their companies dictated.

At first, salesmen sold consumer goods. But through the '40s to '60s, retailers and mail-order companies radically reduced the role of the consumer products salesman – think of the Willy Loman character in *Death of a Salesman*. Salesmen were no longer a cost-effective way for consumer companies to sell their goods, and so the sales role in B2C was radically reduced.

In B2B, however, the role of the salesperson grew during this period. For the sale of expensive and complex machines or parts, salesmen were essential. Large companies invested heavily in their sales forces and developed extensive training programs to teach standardized methods for probing, overcoming objections, and the all-important skill of closing. The era of the product salesman had arrived – Xerox made its reputation as a sales powerhouse in these years for its highly developed sales training programs and methodologies.

As B2B buyers' needs changed over the '70s and '80s, the sales role kept evolving. Some companies found that their highly trained product salespeople started to underperform. The coveted skills of probing, objection-handling, and closing stopped being a perfect recipe for success. A groundbreaking study that became the underpinning of the well-known sales book SPIN Selling (the methodology known as Solution Selling) was conducted by Neil Rackham and his team of 10,000 salespeople. It showed that the traditional sales skills were no longer effective and that a new attribute – *the quality of the questions asked by the salesperson* – was the new key to effective selling.[5] The next era of revenue generation – Consultative (or Solution) Selling – began.

---

5   Rackham, Neil. SPIN Selling. New York: McGraw-Hill, 1988.

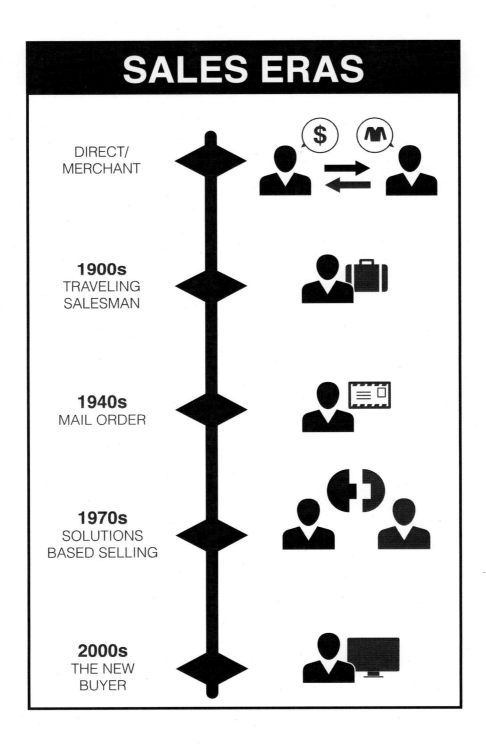

SALES ERAS

DIRECT/
MERCHANT

1900s
TRAVELING
SALESMAN

1940s
MAIL ORDER

1970s
SOLUTIONS
BASED SELLING

2000s
THE NEW
BUYER

Solution Selling has been the focus for many B2B companies for the last twenty years. But just as the era of mass distribution and retailers made Willy Loman less effective, times are once again changing.

In a study conducted from 2009 onwards on sales effectiveness, CEB evaluated the performance of over 6,000 B2B salespeople in eighty-three companies across all major industries. In their article in *Harvard Business Review*, "The End of Solution Sales,"[6] Brent Adamson, Matthew Dixon, and Nicholas Toman share the study's findings and suggest exactly what the title indicates – the era of Solution Selling is over, and a new type of salesperson and selling is on the rise.

> The era of *Solution Selling* is over, and a new type of selling is on the rise.

We are now transitioning from Solution Selling to the *next era* of selling. The reason for the shift is a radical change in buyer behavior. There is a new purchasing process, in which the buyer has much more information and control. As a result, a new approach to generating revenue is necessary. And a big part of that new approach is marketing.

Before we look at the specifics of the new era of selling, let's take a quick look at how we got here and the technological changes that brought the New Buyer into existence.

---

6   http://bit.ly/1sVFtt3

CHAPTER *Two*

How Technology Created the New Buyer

Where did this New Buyer, who takes much more control of the buying process, come from? She's the product of changing times and her behavior has everything to do with technology. There are literally hundreds of tools that enable the New Buyer. Some of those technologies have had more of an impact than others. I've compiled a top ten list of the ones I feel have had the most impact:

1. **Google** (and other search engines)

    When it's time to make a business purchase, 71% of B2B buyers now turn to a search engine first.[7] And that percentage increases every year. What used to happen through word-of-mouth, cold calls and trade shows now happens through Google. There is no greater single change, other than the Internet itself, in how buyers buy. And search is just one facet of the changes that Google has brought about. Other tools within the Google portfolio – including YouTube, Alerts, Analytics, and Adwords – have radically empowered buyers to obtain information whenever they want it.

    Google is now the tradeshow.

    ---

    7   http://bit.ly/1qjVIBy

Google has also radically altered how sellers behave. It provides a previously impossible view into how buyers are behaving and much greater understanding of what buyers are interested in, what messages resonate with them, and what formats of sales and educational materials are most effective.

2. LinkedIn

Facebook may have changed the social world, but it's LinkedIn that is the game changer in B2B. With LinkedIn, buyers can check the backgrounds of salespeople they are interacting with to determine whether they consider them credible. They learn where salespeople have worked and what expertise they bring to the table.

And for sellers, LinkedIn is a treasure trove of information – updated regularly by the buyers themselves, reducing reliance on lists from third parties that are often poor quality. Salespeople use LinkedIn to gain insight on a buyer's role within their organization and their professional background, helping them understand the experience and perspective of the prospects they're working with, the structure of teams and personnel within the target company, and the likely competitive hot buttons.

LinkedIn also provides ready-built forums and communities where professionals can share expertise and perspectives on particular issues – a great way to get on the radar of potential buyers.

3. Email

Email has remade the workday. The average North American office worker spends almost a third of their work week managing email.[8]

---

8   http://bit.ly/1w1IsU7

The average North American office worker spends *28%* of their work week, or 13 hours, managing email.

When it comes to selling, email is now critical to success. Email is the way companies stay on the radar of prospects and customers, gain upsell and cross-sell opportunities, and nurture leads. No salespeople stop by for a visit or even pick up the phone now – they use email.

4. PowerPoint (and other presentation software)

PowerPoint and other presentation software is involved in almost every initial sales meeting. When I speak with salespeople who were active in the '80s, they tell me stories of lugging around slide projectors to sales presentations. I've seen those machines, but never used them. So I'm thankful for that particular change in the way selling happens.

I think there's change on the horizon for the use of PowerPoint. As more and more buyers are doing their homework online, and companies are getting better at providing general information through their websites and other digital publishing tools, the need for the typical "dog and pony show" (a company overview presentation) is declining. I'm sure many capable salespeople will be happy to forgo a PowerPoint presentation in the future and instead move directly into more strategic discussions with prospects.

5. PDF

Though old hat today, the ability to share information seamlessly is in large part due to the PDF platform. Just a decade ago it was a minor technological feat to distribute information that was compatible with all computers. Now, every company can provide PDF case studies for download from their website and have all of their brochures, spec sheets, and other product and service information available in easily shareable documents.

6. YouTube (and other online video hosts)

The average Internet user is exposed to over thirty-two videos every month.[9] And video is still in the early stages of use for businesses. YouTube is the second largest search engine[10] and increasingly buyers use it to find educational videos for products they're researching. For sellers, video is a tremendous opportunity that hasn't yet been harnessed in B2B. With its ability to verbally and visually explain complex products and services, video makes it much easier for B2B companies to educate prospects on what they're offering. It also makes it easier to provide "how to," FAQ, and training videos, which are critical to customer service and the adoption of new products and services.

> The average Internet user views more than
> *32 videos* every month – and climbing.

7. Online Meetings

Tools like GotoMeeting and GotoWebinar make it easy for buyers and sellers to connect, especially when long distances are involved. Buyers worry less about doing business with providers who aren't in their city or country now that online community tools enable them to build relationships and effectively manage projects remotely.

For sellers, online meetings make it much easier to acquire and serve customers outside their local area. A salesperson based in San Francisco

---

9   http://bit.ly/1w1lwmP

10   http://bit.ly/1qjW37q

who's selling across North America can set up initial conversations with potential buyers online. While face-to-face meetings remain the ultimate sales tool, online meeting technologies are reshaping how and with whom we do business.

8. Blogs

Potential buyers no longer need to contact salespeople in order to find out what a company knows about a particular issue or how they approach a specific problem. Instead, they can read about it on the company's blog. What makes a B2B company special is usually its expertise in how a particular product or service can solve a specific problem. Blogs have revolutionized the ability to share that expertise, quickly and efficiently, with a global market.

9. The Cloud

Our ability to access all of our information at any time, and share it with anyone, has exploded with the growth of the cloud in the last five years. Be it document management systems, contact management systems, or any other forms of virtual storage, the cloud has enabled and simplified the sharing of information. For buyers, this has created an expectation of instant information. They don't expect it to be difficult for someone to provide a spec sheet, product overview detail, or any other information the buyer seeks. For sellers, it means that being able to deliver information that was once kept behind corporate firewalls is now the price of entry for engaging the buyer.

10. Online Contracting

There's a growing world of short-term, project-based contracting and freelancing. Whether it's 99designs, Elance, Fiverr or other platforms, our ability to parcel out work and find people around the world who can do that work in a way that is fast and cost-effective is growing rapidly. We are seeing a transformation of the workforce towards more flexible, short-term, contract-based arrangements where companies can find individuals with the specific expertise they need. Every year I see growth in the number of freelancers with knowledge in niche areas who are contracted by my company to deliver that knowledge.

For buyers, the expectation now is that it's possible to go online and find somebody who has specific knowledge, contract them for delivery of that knowledge, and then move on to the next problem. The result is much faster cycle times in business and the ability to address and resolve problems quickly when they arise.

There are many more technologies I could include on this list, and I'm sure you have many that you would add. No matter which technologies you think have had the greatest impact, the net result has been a radical shift in how we work. That shift has created the New Buyer. We'll look at her next.

CHAPTER *Three*

Research on the New Buyer

In this chapter, I present some major studies on how buying behavior is changing. For some readers, this research will help build a business case for making an investment in marketing. For others, it will validate individual experiences on how changing buyer behavior is impacting how companies must sell.

Consumer Studies

There have been two major consumer studies in the past five years that provide extensive data and insight on what is changing in buyer behavior. Although these studies focus on consumers, they provide an excellent overview of how buyer behavior is changing in general. I present quick synopses here, and provide links to the full reports in the text as these studies are well worth a read.

Zero Moment of Truth

In a study commissioned by Google, Shopper Sciences collected data from 5,000 buyers about how they made recent purchases in various categories, including auto, health, grocery, travel, and banking.

The findings were published in a report by Google called the "Zero Moment of Truth," or ZMOT, in 2011. The "moment of truth" refers to a framework in consumer marketing that outlines how consumers make purchase decisions. In the traditional model, there is a stimulus which causes a consumer to want or need a particular product. Then, there are two "moments of truth." The first moment happens at the shelf in a retailer and the second moment happens when the consumer uses the product.

The Google/Shopper Sciences study revealed that there is now an additional moment of truth – the "Zero Moment of Truth" – that happens before a consumer sees a product in a retail store. ZMOT refers to the research that consumers do after they see an advertisement or another trigger, but before they go in store. There are a number of facets to the ZMOT, everything from visiting a company website or Facebook page to reading reviews to connecting with other consumers through social media.

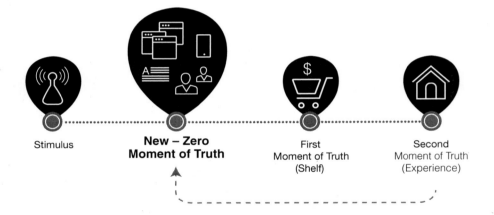

Stimulus

New – Zero Moment of Truth

First Moment of Truth (Shelf)

Second Moment of Truth (Experience)

The ZMOT exerts tremendous influence on what consumers buy. While the amount of influence varies by category, even in the least intensive categories, like grocery, it's over 60%. In categories like automotive and banking, the influence of the ZMOT is over 90%.[11]

There's a range of great findings in the ZMOT study. The full study is available at http://bit.ly/W3qIK7.

---

11   http://bit.ly/W3qIK7

71% of people use the Internet on a **daily** basis for business purchase decisions.

As an addition to the consumer study, Google released a B2B ZMOT. The key statistic in it is simple: 71% of the individuals in the study use the Internet on a <u>daily</u> basis for their business purchase decisions. The Internet is the new trade show.[12]

Consumer Decision Journey

The second important study on buying behavior in the consumer arena is from McKinsey, called the "Consumer Decision Journey."[13] McKinsey reviewed the purchasing decisions of nearly 20,000 consumers across five industries and three continents. They found that the consumer decision-making journey has changed radically. It's no longer a funnel. Today, it's more of a circular, evolving journey, in which the consumer considers and evaluates options throughout the buying process, often looping back to reconsider earlier stages. During the course of buying, consumers pull relevant information when they need it – right up until they make the purchase decision.

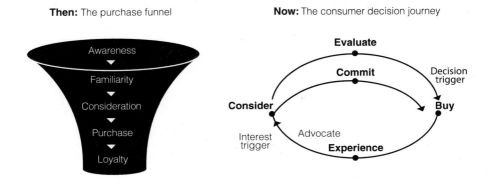

Then: The purchase funnel

Now: The consumer decision journey

---

12   http://bit.ly/1qjVlBy

13   http://bit.ly/1nQjPDd

Like the ZMOT study, the McKinsey research reveals a new landscape for buying. When it comes to how consumers inform themselves during a purchase decision, some radical changes have occurred. Today, only one-third of the sources of information that consumers use in the evaluation phase are company-driven marketing. Two-thirds are third-party information, like Internet reviews, word-of-mouth recommendations, in-store interactions, and recollections of past experiences. That's a radical shift from the days when companies had complete control over their brands.

That said, company-driven marketing is still the most influential information for consumers at the initial consideration stage of the purchasing process. Other sources of information become more important later in the process, as shown below.

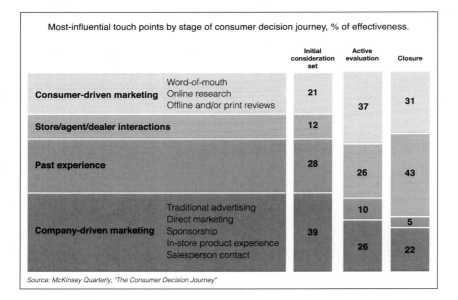

Most-influential touch points by stage of consumer decision journey, % of effectiveness.

		Initial consideration set	Active evaluation	Closure
Consumer-driven marketing	Word-of-mouth Online research Offline and/or print reviews	21	37	31
Store/agent/dealer interactions		12		
Past experience		28	26	43
Company-driven marketing	Traditional advertising Direct marketing Sponsorship In-store product experience Salesperson contact	39	10 26	5 22

Source: McKinsey Quarterly, "The Consumer Decision Journey"

B2B Studies

Both the Google and McKinsey studies provide compelling data on how consumers now make purchasing decisions. Now let's take a look at two studies that reveal the impact of this change in buying behavior in B2B.

The End of Solution Sales

In 2012, CEB published the results of a study conducted among 1,400 B2B customers in an article titled, "The End of Solution Sales,"[14] by Brent Adamson, Matthew Dixon, and Nicholas Toman. This was the research I mentioned earlier that appeared in Harvard Business Review.

Many powerful insights came from the study, but the most compelling finding was that 57% of the typical B2B buying process happens *before* the buyer talks with a single salesperson.

Even in complex sectors, buyers complete almost half (45%) of the purchasing process before they engage with a salesperson. Of twenty-two companies included in the CEB study, none of them had completed less than 45% of the purchasing process before they contacted a salesperson. And none had completed more than 70% of the buying process.

The CEB study highlights that, due to the new buying process, many sales conversations have been turned into fulfillment conversations. As any professional salesperson knows, that drastically limits the ability to provide solutions that deliver good results to the buyer and good profits to the seller.

> Many sales conversations have been turned into *fulfillment* conversations.

Forrester

Forrester has also conducted work in this area, and their results go even further than CEB, finding that buyers are anywhere from 67% to 90% of the way to a decision before they engage a vendor.[15] Buyers now hold off from speaking with salespeople until they're ready for price quotes.

---

14   http://bit.ly/1sVFtt3

15   http://bit.ly/1tUNKQs

These four studies are among many that present a comprehensive view of the changes in buying behavior among both consumers and B2B buyers. The buyer these studies portray is radically different than the buyer of a decade ago. In the next chapter we'll look in detail at this New Buyer.

CHAPTER *Four*

The New Buyer

The buyer of today is vastly different from the buyer of fifteen years ago – even five years ago. The research shows we're in the midst of a buyer revolution – a radical shift toward a new way of buying.

Here are the seven key ways the New Buyer is different from her predecessors and what it means for how she behaves when buying.

1. More Informed

Today's buyer has more information available to her than ever before, and the amount increases every day.

For just about every business problem, no matter how niche or specific, there are dozens of blogs, articles, and other sources of information. Most business searches yield thousands, if not millions, of results that can range from company websites to aficionado blogs. No matter what the question, buyers can find as much information as they want.

> *B2B buyers* today know more about a company's competitors' products than its sales people do.

There is a downside to all this information though. Not all information is reliable. Of all those thousands of blogs, which ones are coming from an objective and expert resource? The challenge for the buyer today is to decipher which information is reliable and which is noise, and which is applicable to her particular situation. It is difficult for the buyer to know.

Despite the challenge of sifting through valid and invalid information, buyers today are substantially more informed than they ever were. They don't wait for presentations from salespeople before identifying solutions to their business problems and determining which solutions are offered by which firms.

In many cases, the B2B buyer today knows more about how a company's offerings stack up against competitors' products than the company's own sales people. Savvy B2B buyers find products and services, learn about them online, compare them with competitors, seek out references from others who've worked with each company, and read online reviews – all before they ever engage with a salesperson. And when buyers do connect with vendors, they're better prepared. They're often ready to jump straight to a quote or pricing – or at least, they think they are.

2.   More Connected

Thanks to technology, the New Buyer is more connected than ever before. She no longer relies on cable to connect to the Internet – she has wifi and her mobile network. She's often on the go, which means she accesses information through a tablet or smart phone. So companies need fast websites that are easy to access from mobile devices.

The New Buyer is also connected to a myriad of information sources. She's good at finding information online, which means she'll look at everything: the LinkedIn profiles and group comments of vendors' teams, the industry associations they belong to, their job postings, user reviews, social media presences, and websites.

Companies tend to think their websites are the only places buyers search – but with the New Buyer, that's rarely the case. And for companies that haven't focused on search engine optimization, it's quite likely third-party sites will rank higher than the company's own website — making this external information the prospect's first impression of the company.

3. More Impatient

B2B buyers have become more impatient. They've grown used to instant gratification because of the Internet.

> Firms who contact prospects within *an hour* of receiving a query are **60x more likely** to have a meaningful conversation with a decision maker than those who wait a day to respond.

The New Buyer wants information quickly — *immediately* in most cases. If a company's website is slow, the buyer will leave in favor of a faster moving site — after all, she has dozens to choose from. Equally, if she can't find the information she's looking for quickly and easily, she'll move on. This means that companies need to reply to customer inquiries and provide quotes and proposals faster than they did even three years ago. Firms that try to contact potential customers within one hour of receiving an online query are over six times more likely to have a meaningful conversation with a key decision maker than those who wait two hours — and more than sixty times as likely as companies that wait twenty-four hours or more.[16]

Once the buyer has determined that she's found the right service or product, she wants to move on to the next step immediately. Empowered buyers want what they want, when and how they want it. Companies need to facilitate the

Empowered buyers want what they want, when and how they want it. Companies need to provide a *purchase process* that supports that desire, not impedes it.

16   http://bit.ly/1oyRb99

purchase process for customers rather than force them through a sales process they don't want or need.

The impatient B2B buyer can have a "stop and go" effect on sales, at least from the seller's perspective. Often buyers will do a flurry of research, only to sit and wait while a decision is made in another part of the company, as a result of the numerous stakeholders involved in purchases. What that means for sellers is often being on the receiving end of a "go" decision that comes out of the blue and must be acted upon quickly.

4. More Overloaded

During the 2008/2009 recession, many companies cut staff dramatically. As a result, the remaining staff took on new responsibilities, often in areas where they had less experience. They acquired greater workloads, spanning wider portfolios.

That situation has not really changed in recent years – businesspeople have continued to have a greater breadth of responsibility. As buyers, this means they need to undertake more research to have the ability to make informed buying decisions. And for sellers, it means buyers are more difficult to reach because they are strapped for time and often aren't an apparent buyer based on their title.

5. More Risk Averse

Due in part to the overload and the general increase in pressure within businesses, the B2B buyer today is more at risk than she used to be. It's easy for sellers to forget that a bad buying decision has a far greater impact on the buyer than on the

A bad purchase decision is much riskier for the buyer than the seller. It could cost her job if things don't go well. Buyers are understandably risk averse.

seller. A purchase mistake could cost the buyer her job, potentially those of her colleagues, and even the success of the business. The New Buyer is more risk averse than the buyer of a decade ago.

6.　More Abundant

The new B2B buying process doesn't involve *a* buyer – it involves *many* buyers. Because of the risks involved in B2B purchases, buyers engage more of their colleagues in the decision in order to avoid a mistake – or at least the perception of a mistake – and to spread the risk.

According to a 2013 study by CSO Insight,[17] over 46% of B2B purchases involve more than four individuals in the final decision. More stakeholders means more buying complexity. Sellers have to not only identify each stakeholder, they also need to address each party's needs, priorities, and concerns, and find a selling approach that's reasonable with each. This requires more skill and more resources.

7.　More Autonomous

As the research shows, buyers want to delay speaking with sales representatives until as late in the purchasing process as possible. They want to do their own research, make their own evaluations, and work on their own schedules. Increasingly, this means working outside regular business hours, like during evenings and weekends. The New Buyer wants to be as self-sufficient and independent as possible.

17　　http://bit.ly/1luHCwU

In summary, here are the seven factors that make New Buyers radically different from their predecessors. New Buyers are:

1. More informed
2. More connected
3. More impatient
4. More overloaded
5. More risk averse
6. More abundant
7. More autonomous

These differences are causing a radical shift in the buying process. And when the buying process is radically different, selling needs to be radically different too.

In Part Two, I'll discuss three areas where the New Buyer is having the biggest impact on how B2B companies generate revenue.

PART TWO

WHAT THE NEW BUYER MEANS FOR SELLING

This section presents several areas where new buying behavior is radically altering the approach that B2B companies take to generating revenue. It outlines how companies who rethink their pipeline, sales team structure, resources, and the role of marketing in their business can achieve radical improvements.

CHAPTER *Five*

New Revenue Generation Thinking

Many companies are finding that their traditional approach to generating revenue – namely through their sales team – isn't working as well as it used to. The processes they've used in the past are generating weaker results each year, and many of the structures, tools, and frameworks they've been using are now misaligned with how buyers buy.

The reason for this is the New Buyer. The way the New Buyer buys is having a radical impact on how well B2B companies generate revenue. The impact is felt in many ways, and B2B companies who change how they sell are able to grow their revenues and profits rather than watch them flatline. There are three ways that B2B companies are changing their revenue-generation activities to match how the New Buyer buys:

1. **The New Pipeline** – The "sales funnel" is less accurate in depicting the buying and selling process today; now the buying process is more like a pinball machine.

2. **A New Sales Approach** – Salespeople need to up their game to be valuable to the New Buyer.

3. **The Growing Role of Marketing** – Because half the buying process is done before a buyer talks to anyone in sales, marketing has to fulfill activities at the front end of the buying process.

Let's look at these changes one by one.

CHAPTER Six

The New Pipeline

Sales organizations have used the funnel to represent the buying process for decades. It was introduced in 1898 by Elias St. Elmo Lewis.[18] It's now widely accepted, and just about everyone in sales has used the funnel with some variation in its phases. Here are some variations on the funnel:

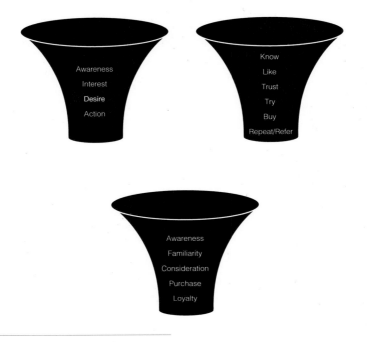

---

18 Strong, Edward K. *The Psychology of Selling and Advertising.* New York: McGraw-Hill Book, 1925. 349 and 9. Print.

In the traditional funnel, customers enter at the top and progress in a linear direction towards the bottom, which denotes a purchase. There's a conversion rate at each stage of the funnel, i.e. some customers will transition to the next stage of the funnel, and some won't. Forecasting is done on the basis of the company knowing its conversion rates and calculating the amount of potential and likely business at each stage of the funnel.

But as the research has shown, the traditional funnel isn't an accurate reflection of the buying process now. Customers pursue a more circular purchasing journey now and can just as easily bounce from one stage to the next, go back to an earlier stage, and then go straight to purchase.

> *Customers* have a more circular purchasing journey now. They can appear to slide from one stage to the next, bounce back to an earlier stage, and then leap straight to purchase.

Due to this seemingly erratic purchasing journey, I think the new B2B buying process is better depicted as a pinball machine.

Imagine a typical pinball machine. The balls enter from one side and must navigate a variety of bumpers and gates to reach the goal at the top of the playing surface. At a few places there are gutters that, when the ball enters them, cause the ball to fall back to the starting point – or out of the game entirely.

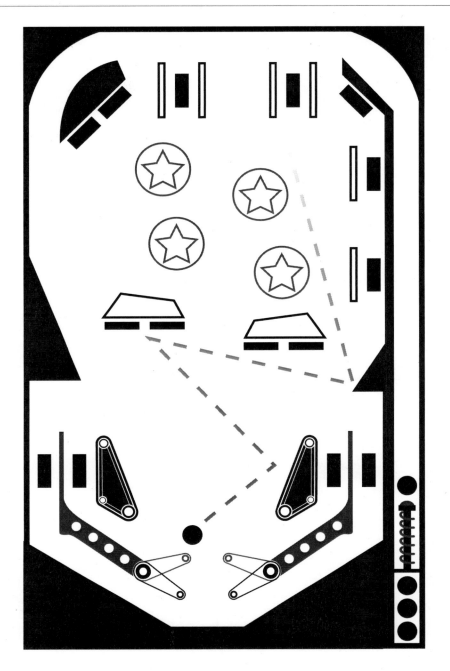

In the pinball analogy of the purchasing process, the lead generation activities represent the entrance to the board, and the gates, bumpers, and obstacles on the surface represent sales and marketing tactics – everything from factory tours to webinars to free trials. And the goal at the top is when the prospect becomes a customer. The prospect in this analogy is the ball.

Sellers can attract balls to the board through their marketing and they can control where the gates and bumpers are placed. They can't, however, control how each ball will react to the gates and bumpers.

Sellers will recognize the new reality of the sales process in the pinball analogy. For example, imagine a ball that enters the playing surface and, based on its initial trajectory, looks like it will head straight for the goal – but instead, it hits a particular gate and goes in the opposite direction of what the seller expected.

Conversely, every once in a while, a ball will hit a certain gate and go right into the goal. Other times, it will enter the board, hit a dozen paddles and then drop to the gutter unexpectedly. That's how purchasing is these days. Once in a while, a buyer will come in and make a purchase within one or two conversations. In other situations it feels like there's progress towards the goal, and then something happens. The prospect hits a wall or their momentum changes for a reason unknown to the seller, and the deal is lost.

Sometimes there are eighteen steps between a ball entering the playing surface and it going through the goal, and sometimes there are three.

Despite the variety of interactions that balls have with the playing surface, the pinball machine is not random. Its gates and bumpers, and the movement of the ball on the playing surface, are governed by the laws of physics. The reason it can seem random is because there are many variables affecting every game – the size and density of the ball, its trajectory, and the angle at which it hits gates and paddles. Taken together, there's too much happening for it to be easily understood.

But in the pinball analogy, the seller *can* control one thing: the set-up of the playing surface. The seller can create the gates and paddles (sales and marketing tactics) and where they're located. This means that, with careful attention, the seller can place gates and paddles in locations where they are most effective in sending the ball towards the goal.

I like the pinball analogy for depicting the buying process because it illustrates the seemingly random nature of the process – when in fact, there is science behind the machine and how it works.

> The pinball analogy conveys the seemingly random *nature of buying* (although it isn't) and illustrates how diligent sellers can put the right interactions in place to increase sales.

I also like the pinball analogy because it conveys that sellers can control the touches and interactions (gates and bumpers) that buyers will experience, even if they can't control how buyers will react. But over time, if sellers are diligent in measuring and monitoring, they can identify which gates and bumpers send prospects towards the goal, and put more of those in place.

CHAPTER Seven

A New Sales Approach

The second major implication of the New Buyer is that B2B companies need to adjust their sales approach. This can affect everything from the sales process to the types of people recruited for sales roles.

When Neil Rackham studied sales effectiveness among thousands of salespeople in the '70s, he learned that a different set of skills was needed to sell solutions than had been necessary to sell products. The approach that product salespeople had used for the previous two decades, when handling objections and focusing on closing, rendered those salespeople much less productive when it came to the emerging buyer of the time, who had complex issues. What makes a Solution Salesperson effective is his or her ability to ask questions that clarify a buyer's business situation, articulate the implications of particular problems, and present solutions to those problems – the classic SPIN model presented in Rackham's 1988 book, *SPIN Selling.*[19]

Now buyers are changing again and the SPIN model is less effective. Buyers aren't engaging with salespeople until they've completed their own needs assessment and more than half of the purchasing process. This means sales often doesn't have the ability to ask questions, articulate implications, and present solutions for a client's needs.

---

19   Rackham, Neil. *SPIN Selling*. New York: McGraw-Hill, 1988.

Today, the skills that make for a great salesperson have to do with leading and coaching customers with insights, so that the customer can see what problems they have (or might soon have) and how they should address them. Matthew Dixon and Brent Abramson have done extensive research to profile a new, more effective seller, which they present in their book, *The Challenger Sale: Taking Control of the Customer Conversation.*[20]

To be effective now, B2B salespeople need deep business and technical acumen combined with sales skills. Because buyers are gathering more information about the products and services they purchase prior to contacting suppliers, they're well-informed by the time they speak with a sales rep and are looking for a significantly deeper level of knowledge and expertise from salespeople.

The New Buyer has raised the bar for the sales team.

As a result, sales people now need to understand both the technical aspects of what they're selling *and* how it applies to particular business situations. They also need to be able to calibrate quickly to each individual buyer's needs, assess a buyer's level of understanding, and progress the conversation from there.

Less experienced sales reps can make the mistake of using a specific sales process and trying to force a buyer to a particular starting point. This usually frustrates the buyer to the degree that they disengage. More effective sales reps are able to ask a few questions to ascertain where the buyer is at in their process. Then they provide the answers, and likely generate discussion that demonstrates their expertise and their ability to add value. From there, the seller has gained credibility and some control over the sales process.

Because of this shift in the type of skills that make for effective salespeople, many B2B companies, especially those with complex and technical solutions, are finding that junior salespeople struggle to achieve their targets. They lack the technical and application knowledge to be able to add value for customers. For this reason, many companies are shifting the elements of their early sales

20   http://bit.ly/1qwyG9m

process to their marketing function, and refining their sales team to retain senior salespeople who have the ability to add value for prospects and convert leads into customers.

Other companies are reshaping the structure of their sales organization to account for different skill levels and customers at different stages of the buying journey. As Aaron Ross describes in his book *Predictable Revenue*, a segmented approach is proving extremely effective for some businesses. Rather than have a single sales person responsible for shepherding a customer from the beginning through end of the purchase journey, different members of the sales team (with different skill levels) are in place. Outbound reps are responsible for doing outreach, inbound reps handle all incoming inquiries and triage leads to determine which should be passed on to more experienced reps. This structure allows for development of sales team members, and for prospects to get the level of sales expertise they need, when they need it.

CHAPTER *Eight*

The Growing
Role of Marketing

The first two areas I've covered – rethinking the pipeline and adapting the sales team structure – focus on changing the existing ways that most B2B companies operate. This next area is often something entirely new for B2B companies: marketing.

A decade ago, marketing wasn't an essential business function for mid-market B2B companies. Due to their targeted customer bases, the traditional means of marketing – like TV commercials and billboards – didn't make financial sense. So trade shows and the odd print advertisement in trade publications became the only marketing tactics for B2B companies. Even though sales reps were a relatively expensive way to generate revenues, B2B companies didn't have feasible alternatives and relied on the sales team as the primary route to raising awareness, generating leads, and securing revenue.

Today, the Internet has radically changed that. Because the New Buyer conducts half or more of the purchasing process online, B2B companies have more cost-effective ways to get their message out to potential customers. And because of increasing competition and shrinking margins, B2B companies have to take advantage of these new, less expensive ways to generate awareness and leads through marketing.

marketing is now an important function for B2B companies, and companies are implementing a marketing function. The companies who recognize that marketing can play an important role in the success of their business look for marketing to make an impact in these five areas:

1.   Defining Strategy

A marketing strategy articulates where and how a company will compete. This entails decisions on value proposition, target markets and positioning. (See sidebar – "What's in a Marketing Strategy?")

2.   Raising Market Awareness

Marketing's job is to ensure the company is known by potential customers. B2B companies that are recognized by prospects are three times more likely to be selected as a vendor. Every sales person benefits when a prospect has already heard of his or her company and products.

3.   Generating Leads

Leads can be generated by undertaking marketing activities and tactics that attract potential customers. This entails utilizing a growing number of marketing tools, like webinars and pay-per-click advertising. When combined with strong market awareness, lead generation campaigns provide highly measurable ROI.

4.   Supporting Sales

Marketing has an important role to play in ensuring the sales team is as productive and successful as possible. By providing collateral and other tools, marketing allows the sales team to spend their time engaged directly with prospects.

5. Increasing Retention and Share of Wallet

Marketing can create and manage programs that ensure customers understand the full breadth of products and services the company offers, so that customers do more business with the company each year.

Marketing is like a chain – it's only as strong as its weakest link. Companies need to address each of the five areas in relatively even proportion – they shouldn't focus only on one area to the exclusion of all the others if they want high-performance revenue generation.

And one important thing to consider – everything I've described above relates to customers, but there's another side to marketing that has nothing to do with customers, and that's *attracting new staff*. Many B2B companies will be facing significant turnover of staff in the next decade. They're already struggling with the reality of needing to attract the next generation of engineers, designers, planners, and skilled trades people. What's the first thing someone under thirty-five does when they hear about a job opportunity? They go online to investigate the company. A company with a weak online presence may be suffering not just in their ability to attract new customers, but also in their ability to

WHAT'S IN A *Marketing Strategy?*

Often, marketing strategy is described as "The 4 Ps" – Product, Price, Place (distribution) and Promotion. In my experience, most B2B companies already have their Product, Price and Place determined. The more useful elements to include in a marketing strategy for B2B companies are:

1. **VALUE PROPOSITION**: What are you selling and why should buyers buy from you? What unique factors does your company have that are important to customers? The more specific, objective, and quantified your answer, the better. Value proposition is also described as USP (unique selling proposition) or competitive advantage.

2. **TARGET MARKETS**: Who are your ideal customers? What needs and priorities do they have? B2B companies can't be all things to all customers. The more you focus on a specific segment of the market, the more successful you'll be. Most B2B companies should pursue more than one target market, but fewer than five (large companies with extensive sales and marketing teams can serve more).

3. **POSITIONING**: What is the specific and desired understanding of your company in the minds of your target customers? A positioning statement defines how a company wants to be known to its target customers — it is the company's desired reputation.

attract the next generation of talent for the business.

By now, you have a good picture of the New Buyer and how changes in buying behavior are radically changing how B2B companies generate revenues. In Part Three, there are three diagnostic tools to help you evaluate your current marketing and sales functions, and the integration of the two.

PART THREE

DIAGNOSTICS

This section has three diagnostic tools to help you evaluate where to focus your time and attention. Some companies have flat revenues because they lack marketing, some have a weak sales process, and others have sales and marketing functions that aren't well aligned. The diagnostics will help you identify where the problems are and how to improve your revenue engine.

CHAPTER *Nine*

Introduction to Marketing and Sales Diagnostics

To help companies identify how best to improve their revenue generation, Part Three contains three diagnostic tools. The first tool is a B2B marketing diagnostic. Because marketing is a new function for many B2B companies, there are often gaps here that affect revenue generation. Most business leaders won't be surprised by the results of this diagnostic – they already know whether they have work to do in marketing. This tool provides insight and guidance on where to focus their efforts.

The second tool is a B2B sales diagnostic. Companies might be surprised by their results here. I've seen many successful B2B companies who lack a well-structured sales function. These companies have become successful without needing to be especially disciplined with their sales organization because they've had strong relationships in their industry, or products and services that competitors couldn't match, or they are simply entrenched in their customers' businesses and there has been no impetus for change.

Over *90%* of mid-market B2B companies don't have a structured sales process.

In fact the majority of mid-market B2B companies – many of whom consider their sales organization relatively effective – operate this way. According to a study of 50,000 salespeople by Objective

Management Group, 91%[21] of mid-market B2B companies don't have a structured, formal sales process. Some companies have a revenue goal, but it isn't broken down by sales rep. Others don't have a structured sales process with defined stages of the purchase process. Many companies don't have a CRM system that allows them to capture data on the sales process and understand the conversion rate from one stage of the purchasing process to the next.

B2B companies who have gaps in their sales function should consider addressing these issues first – before they add marketing, or at least alongside marketing. Marketing will increase awareness and lead generation, which might only exacerbate weaknesses in the sales function.

And finally there's a diagnostic for the integration of sales and marketing. These two functions are interwoven, and for effective B2B revenue generation, they must work closely together. There's a growing sentiment that in B2B companies, the sales and marketing teams will increasingly be merged into a single "revenue department." That hasn't happened yet in most B2B companies, so in the interim this diagnostic will help identify where the two teams can improve their communications and collaboration.

---

21   http://bit.ly/1BkUrOG

CHAPTER Ten

B2B Marketing Diagnostic

For decades, the sales team was the revenue engine for B2B companies. Today, marketing has a serious role to play when it comes to increasing sales. This diagnostic helps you identify where your marketing is performing well, and where you should enhance your efforts.

Instructions

The Marketing Diagnostic has five components. For each question, give your company a score of 0 – 4 based on the scale below.

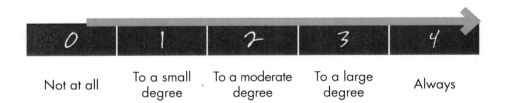

0	1	2	3	4
Not at all	To a small degree	To a moderate degree	To a large degree	Always

MARKETING STRATEGY

SCORE 0 – 4

1. Our employees know and can explain how we're different from other companies in our industry.

2. We understand who our ideal customers are and why they use us.

3. We understand how our target customers make buying decisions for our products or services.

4. We're clear in our message about what makes us different and why customers should use us.

5. Our customers understand fully what we do and how we're different from other companies.

STRATEGY SUBTOTAL

0	1	2	3	4
Not at all	To a small degree	To a moderate degree	To a large degree	Always

MARKET AWARENESS

SCORE 0 - 4

1. We are known by target customers as a reliable company in our industry.

2. We are invited or accepted to speak at industry conferences and client sessions.

3. We get sole-sourced for new business.

4. We are able to achieve premium pricing against other solutions that prospects may be considering.

5. We regularly share our expertise through thought leadership (articles, white papers, case studies, infographics) via in-person and digital channels.

MARKET AWARENESS SUBTOTAL

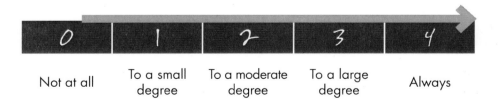

0	1	2	3	4
Not at all	To a small degree	To a moderate degree	To a large degree	Always

LEAD GENERATION

SCORE 0 - 4

1. We know the keywords (search terms) that people use to find information online about the problems we solve.

2. We integrate those keywords into our content to ensure we rank well on search engines.

3. We publish press releases and have relationships with key media to get industry attention for our company.

4. We have a blog and publish new posts regularly.

5. We network at events where our prospects and customers (not just our industry peers) gather.

LEAD GENERATION SUBTOTAL

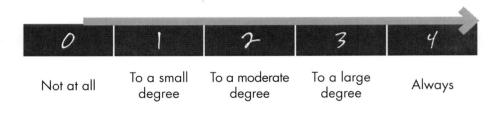

0	1	2	3	4
Not at all	To a small degree	To a moderate degree	To a large degree	Always

SALES SUPPORT

1. Our sales team has effective, standardized collateral that helps them present our offerings.

2. We have case studies, ROI calculators, and other materials that our sales team uses to help prospects progress from one stage of the purchase process to the next.

3. We use a CRM system.

4. We stay in touch with prospects who are not yet ready to buy through opt-in email communications.

5. Our sales and marketing teams meet at least every two weeks to discuss initiatives and performance.

SALES SUPPORT SUBTOTAL

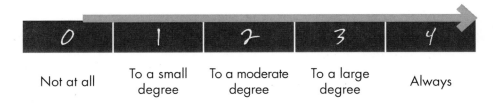

0	1	2	3	4
Not at all	To a small degree	To a moderate degree	To a large degree	Always

CUSTOMER RETENTION & GROWTH

SCORE 0 – 4

1. We communicate regularly with past customers. ☐

2. We undertake a customer satisfaction assessment or customer advisory council at least every other year. ☐

3. We grow the amount of business we do with our existing customer base by 5% per year or more. ☐

4. Our customers refer new business to us. ☐

5. We do repeat business with the majority of our most profitable customers. ☐

CUSTOMER RETENTION & GROWTH SUBTOTAL ☐

TOTAL SCORE (ALL 5 SECTIONS) ☐

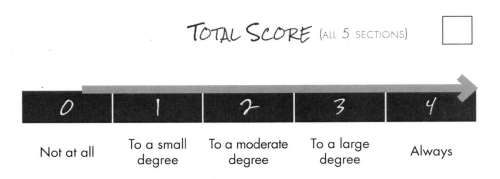

0	1	2	3	4
Not at all	To a small degree	To a moderate degree	To a large degree	Always

B2B Marketing Diagnostic

Under 20: Marketing Neophyte

You have great opportunities to use marketing to drive sales for your business. Start by establishing a good foundation (marketing strategy). Then focus on the areas where you have the biggest opportunities – often sales support and customer retention and growth provide the most immediate marketing ROI.

Building effective marketing isn't a quick process. When you're starting to put marketing to work, you should see progress within six months, but revenue results – especially if the buying cycle in your industry is long – will take longer. It takes most companies over two years to achieve highly effective and efficient marketing. To get there, you'll have to make a long-term commitment and have the patience to see initiatives through. If you do, you can radically transform your revenue engine.

21 – 40: Marketing Junior

Great work – you've started to put marketing to work in your business. Your score indicates you may be tackling it ad hoc rather than holistically. If your section score for marketing strategy is strong, that's good – you have a foundation in place. If not, spend more time on strategy rather than on individual marketing campaigns and projects so that you'll see better results over the long term. If your strategy is strong but you have weak scores across the other four areas (market awareness, lead generation, sales support, and customer retention and growth), focus on the area where you're weakest and make improvements there. Balance your efforts across the four areas to get to a moderate level in each — effective marketing is typically balanced across the four functions rather than very strong in one area and weak in the others.

41 – 65: Marketing Senior

You're on the path to powerful marketing. You have a reasonably strong score in marketing strategy and are executing moderately in the other four areas (market awareness, lead generation, sales support, and customer retention and growth). To elevate the impact that marketing has, review your scores in each of the four sections and identify the single lowest score. This will be the area where you have the best opportunity to make enhancements that will drive results. Create your action plan to implement initiatives that will raise the score of this section to within a few points of your highest scoring section. Then repeat the process until you've graduated to "Marketing Sophisticate."

65+: Marketing Sophisticate

Congratulations, you are putting marketing to work. You've established a strong foundation (marketing strategy) and are executing a comprehensive marketing plan that covers all the core areas (market awareness, lead generation, sales support, and customer retention and growth). There are likely areas that can benefit from enhancements, but overall you know what they are and are tackling them in order of priority. As you think about where to go next in marketing, review your answers and focus on the specific areas that score the lowest. Elevate these lowest scores to enhance the power of marketing on your revenue and profit engine.

CHAPTER *Eleven*

B2B Sales Diagnostic

There's clear evidence that companies with a formal sales process generate more revenue. But almost half of executives feel that their organizations are ineffective at managing their own sales process.[22] This sales diagnostic helps you identify how your sales function is performing, and where you should enhance your efforts.

Instructions

The Sales Diagnostic has four components. For each question, give your company a score of 0 – 4 based on the scale below.

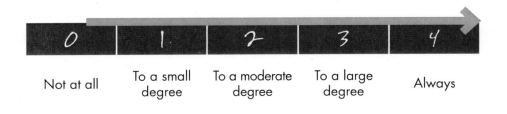

0	1	2	3	4
Not at all	To a small degree	To a moderate degree	To a large degree	Always

---

22   http://bit.ly/1LD6QDs

SALES RECRUITING AND TRAINING

SCORE 0 - 4

1. Our employees know and can explain how we're different from other companies in our industry. ☐

2. We understand who our ideal customers are and why they use us. ☐

3. We conduct sales training and sharing of best practices among team members twice a year or more. ☐

4. A sales manager spends a half a day each month or more doing active coaching with each sales rep. ☐

RECRUITING & TRAINING SUBTOTAL ☐

0	1	2	3	4
Not at all	To a small degree	To a moderate degree	To a large degree	Always

SALES PROCESS AND SKILLS

SCORE 0 - 4

1. We have scripts, presentations, proposals, and other templates to maintain consistency and reduce the amount of time that sales reps spend creating materials.

2. We have a defined pipeline with clear stages and criteria for progressing from one stage to the next.

3. When someone calls our office, it is easy for them to speak with an appropriate sales representative.

4. We follow up on all new leads within a single business day.

5. We have an established and clear pricing matrix that allows reps to quickly generate quotes.

6. We provide salespeople with industry insight they can leverage in conversations with customers.

7. We use a CRM system consistently and effectively.

8. Our sales team members have deep technical knowledge that enables them to close deals.

9.   Our sales team members are capable of having conversations with senior customer executives and coming up with solutions to their business problems.

☐

10.   We have a clear process to transition leads from one member of the sales team to another when appropriate.

☐

SALES PROCESS AND SKILLS SUBTOTAL ☐

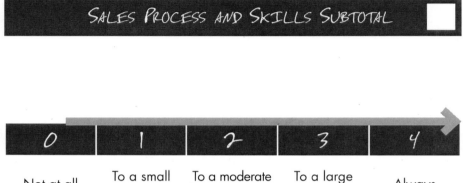

0	1	2	3	4
Not at all	To a small degree	To a moderate degree	To a large degree	Always

MANAGEMENT AND MEASUREMENT

SCORE 0 - 4

1. We have a quota for each sales team member.

2. We do key account planning and territory management on an annual basis.

3. Each sales rep meets with their manager on a weekly or bi-weekly basis to discuss their pipeline.

4. Our senior leadership team consistently looks at sales reports, from the forecast to conversion metrics to individual sales rep reports.

5. We have a structured compensation system tied to quotas.

MANAGEMENT AND MEASUREMENT SUBTOTAL

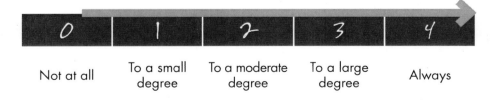

0	1	2	3	4
Not at all	To a small degree	To a moderate degree	To a large degree	Always

PERFORMANCE OVERALL

SCORE 0 - 4

1. We can accurately predict new rep success based on number of leads and average conversion metrics.

2. At least 80% of our sales team meet quota every year.

3. We can accurately forecast sales using the data that sales reps provide.

4. We understand our target conversion rate from one stage of the pipeline to the next.

5. We have clearly defined growth metrics that we assess often (e.g. average deal size, pipeline generated per month).

PERFORMANCE OVERALL SUBTOTAL

TOTAL SCORE (ALL 5 SECTIONS)

0	1	2	3	4
Not at all	To a small degree	To a moderate degree	To a large degree	Always

B2B Sales

Under 20: Sales Neophyte

The sales function in your organization is largely unstructured. If you have multiple sales people, this situation probably arose because your industry has been relationship driven, or because the members of your senior sales team have been with your organization a long time and are autonomous and self-motivated. In short, you've been lucky. But as markets become more competitive and buyer behaviour changes, your sales organization will need to change as well.

If your sales process and skills score is low (less than 18), this is the area to address first as it will bring the biggest impact. If there are process gaps (like not responding to leads immediately or failing to turn around quotes quickly), identify the resources and processes to fix them. These kinds of changes will demonstrate the company's commitment to improving the sales organization, and will galvanize the sales team to make changes in their own processes. If you do not have a defined sales process, work with the sales team to create it — it can be done in a few hours and will enable the team to have better discussions about individual leads in the future (as long as you hold regular sales meetings and ask about individual leads).

If your score in management and measurement is low, the head of the sales organization can implement changes that will radically improve the discipline of the sales organization. But these changes will need to be carefully communicated and implemented so as not to alienate the sales team (especially if it is long-tenured).

If your score in recruiting and training is low (less than 8), address this problem after tackling the existing, internal issues – because every new rep you bring in is destined to struggle if they aren't the right profile and if they don't have support.

Bringing structure and discipline to a sales organization is difficult. Often the skills and knowledge to achieve a well-managed sales organization don't exist within the company. If this is the case, consider engaging an outside sales expert to bring the new structure and processes in.

21 – 40: Sales Junior

You recognize the value of good management and discipline in the sales organization and have begun to put structure and process in place, although in a limited way. Look at your scores in each of the four areas to determine where you've been focused and where more attention and commitment is needed. Choose the areas that are easier to tackle first – for example, fixing processes for lead management and quote preparation. Tackle the harder areas, like quotas, after you've gained momentum through other initiatives.

41 – 65: Sales Senior

You're well on the path to effective sales management. You likely have a reasonably strong score in the first three areas (recruiting and training, sales process and skills, management and measurement). To elevate the success of your sales organization, select three low-scoring statements and make an action plan to address them over the next six months.

65+: Sales Sophisticate

Congratulations, you run a highly disciplined sales organization. You have a strong structure and are managing the sales organization on an ongoing basis. There are likely areas that can benefit from extra attention, but overall you know what they are and are tackling them in order of priority. As you think about further enhancing the performance of your sales team, review your answers and focus on the specific statements that score the lowest. Elevate your scores in these areas to enhance the power of your sales engine.

CHAPTER *Twelve*

B2B Marketing and Sales Integration

Some companies have very strong sales teams and very strong marketing teams – but still struggle to achieve the revenue engine they seek. It's the strength of the two teams, with a lack of integration between them, that causes the problem. This diagnostic will help you evaluate how well your sales and marketing teams work together.

Instructions

The Marketing and Sales Integration Diagnostic has ten questions. For each question, give your company a score of 0 – 4 based on the scale below.

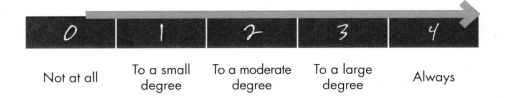

0	1	2	3	4
Not at all	To a small degree	To a moderate degree	To a large degree	Always

B2B MARKETING AND SALES INTEGRATION

SCORE 0 - 4

1   Sales and marketing have jointly developed the customer persona of target buyers. ☐

2   The sales and marketing organizations share a consistent lead-to-revenue model and manage their individual activities based on it. ☐

3   Sales and marketing have created common definitions of key terms like "qualified lead," "deal size," and "customer retention." ☐

4   Sales and marketing know each others' goals and metrics. ☐

5   The heads of the sales and marketing functions develop their plans collaboratively. ☐

6   The marketing team involves the sales team in developing its annual marketing plan. ☐

7   The sales team involves the marketing team in developing its annual sales plan. ☐

8   Sales and marketing meet at least every other week to review new leads, discuss their quality, and update their status in the pipeline.

9   Marketers go on prospect calls with the sales team at least twice a year.

10   Sales and marketing report to a single C-suite executive.

SALES PROCESS AND SKILLS TOTAL

TOTAL SCORE (ALL 5 SECTIONS)

0	1	2	3	4
Not at all	To a small degree	To a moderate degree	To a large degree	Always

SCORE ANALYSIS

Marketing and Sales Integration Analysis

Under 15: Sales and Marketing Silos

The sales and marketing teams in your organization operate primarily in silos, which constrains their effectiveness and limits their combined success. Improved collaboration will start at the top – with the leaders of sales and marketing. If the two leaders don't want to collaborate or don't see the benefit of working together, it will be difficult to make radical improvements. If, however, the two leaders simply haven't identified the benefit of collaboration, the diagnostic is a good starting point for bringing them together.

If the marketing team has never been on sales calls, have them do that within the next four weeks. If your company is about to start its annual planning process, set up joint sessions for sales and marketing to plan together and extract knowledge from each other. And if the two teams don't meet regularly, invite marketing to the next sales meeting – and continue to have them join every meeting in the future.

16 – 30: Sales and Marketing are Good Acquaintances

Your sales and marketing teams have a cooperative relationship and there is good respect between them. However, they aren't fully leveraging the benefits of a deep integration of their activities. Look at the score for each statement and identify where deeper integration or communication will help the two teams work more effectively. If they haven't done so already, have marketing go on sales calls to increase their understanding of customers, encourage sales and marketing to review leads on a weekly basis in order to refine the team's definition of a qualified lead, and during the annual planning process, have sales and marketing collaborate to better leverage key marketing initiatives and time them with customer buying cycles.

30+: Sales and Marketing are Best Friends

Your sales and marketing teams work well together. They plan together, have shared definitions of the customer and the buying process, and communicate frequently in order to consistently react to market changes. Keep up the good work by identifying any specific statements where you score three or lower — these are the areas to consider for attention.

PART FOUR

20 LESSONS FROM 20 LEADERS

Part Four is a road map for building your revenue engine. Twenty phenomenal marketers have shared their expertise and experiences in how to make marketing work for B2B companies. I've shaped their insights into twenty lessons for business owners and marketing leaders on how to apply marketing to generate more revenue and profit for your business.

CHAPTER *Thirteen*

The 20 Leaders

Great B2B marketers are a rare breed. That's because B2B marketing isn't just about marketing – it's about revenue. So great B2B marketers aren't just marketing leaders – they're revenue generation experts. They have expertise that spans all areas of business (from finance to sales to operations), and they use marketing as a tool to achieve business objectives, rather than to achieve marketing objectives.

As marketing grows in importance for B2B companies, there will be more revenue generators and more leaders among their ranks. But right now, I estimate there are around 100 exceptional mid-market B2B revenue generators in Canada – the kinds of people who have deep strategic sales and marketing knowledge, experience managing a wide variety of tactics to achieve revenue goals, and an understanding of the unique environment of small and mid-size B2B companies, which have different operating requirements than enterprise marketing. Thankfully, this number is growing every year.

Twenty of these exceptional B2B revenue generators participated in the development of this book, sharing the expertise and experience they've gained over the last ten to twenty years of their careers.

Here's the roster of the twenty leaders, the environments they operate in, and some of their accomplishments.

The Twenty Leaders (alphabetically listed)

Dawn Abankwah

Dawn is currently vice president of business development at Spafinder Wellness 365™, a media and marketing company for the wellness industry. She is the leader for both B2B and consumer revenue generation for Spafinder in Canada.

Dawn has over a decade of experience driving revenues for B2B organizations. After beginning her career in B2B sales, she joined The Hudson's Bay Company as manager of the company's B2B Gift Card program. Within four years, she was promoted to senior manager of corporate accounts and managed all facets of the company's B2B program, including developing, executing, and managing the business strategy and marketing plan. She moved to StoreFinancial in 2009 where she became director of business development. In 2012, Dawn joined Aimia as a principal consultant within the Client Strategy and Insight team. There, she designed and developed loyalty strategy and programs for the retail and financial verticals while supporting business development as a subject matter expert in consumer and retail loyalty.

Janet Campbell

Janet Campbell has over twenty years of experience as a sales professional in the records and information management industry. Currently, she is the vice-president of sales at TAB Products of Canada. Since joining TAB as an account executive in 1998, Janet's role has expanded from branch manager to regional manager to her current role as a member of TAB's executive leadership team. Prior to joining TAB, Janet spent nearly ten years at Crain-Drummond where her role expanded from sales representative to strategic account executive to business development consultant for the Print Management Services Division responsible for the Western Region. She has served on the Board of Directors for various industry and community associations.

Leslie Carter

Leslie Carter has over twenty years of brand management and marketing experience. Currently, she is the chief brand and strategy officer for Knightsbridge Human Capital Solutions, where she is responsible for corporate strategy, brand management, customer strategy and marketing capabilities, including corporate communications, sponsorships and events, and customer relationship marketing.

Leslie began her career in brand management at Kraft Canada, where she worked for four years before joining Pepsi-Cola. Leslie began her seven-year tenure at Pepsi as marketing manager and later became director of marketing. Leslie went on to work as the vice president of marketing for Swiss Chalet and Harvey's Cara Operations before starting a brand strategy and analytics consulting firm, Brand-Aide, in 2007. Leslie joined Knightsbridge to lead the company's strategic marketing function in 2009. She is a graduate of the University of Toronto and holds a Bachelor of Commerce in marketing and finance.

Christina DiLallo

Christina DiLallo has over ten years of experience in B2B marketing and business development. Currently, she is the marketing manager for Newcomp, an IBM Business Partner and provider of IBM Business Analytics, where she is responsible for the development and implementation of Newcomp's marketing plans.

Over the last four years, she has worked to execute bi-yearly website refreshes, email and social media campaigns, workshops, and trade shows, among other tactics. During her tenure at Newcomp, the company was named IBM Business Analytics Partner of the Year for its focus and dedication to analytics. Previously, Christina was the national account manager for PCM Technologies/PCMusic, a PC-based, on-demand music, video, and AV provider for businesses. Prior to joining PCM, Christina worked for Life Line Manufacturing as a marketing and business development executive.

Christina is a graduate of Ryerson University. She holds a Bachelor of Commerce with a specialization in management.

Mark Fasken

Mark Fasken has spent several years working in business development in B2B companies, focusing on sales strategies for start-ups. He is currently a regional sales manager with Influitive, an advocate marketing company that helps B2B companies harness the power of referrals, product reviews, references and social shares. Mark gained deep experience in achieving sales effectiveness while working with Third Core Venture Expansion Partners, an organization that outsources and fulfills the sales function for start-ups, as well as working in the business development function for Couch & Associates, a marketing consultancy that specializes in marketing automation and effective sales enablement.

Mark is an ambassador for the Sales Hacker Series, which brings together frontline salespeople to explore actionable tactics and strategies. He has also acted as a mentor while working with INcubes, where he helped start-ups establish structured, execution focused sales strategies. Mark holds an Honours BA from Wilfred Laurier University.

Joanne Gore

Joanne Gore has nearly twenty years of marketing and communications experience in both corporate and mid-market environments. Over the course of her career, she has developed lead generation and conversion programs, re-branded product lines, and implemented social media strategies.

A graduate of the Graphic Design program at Dawson College in Montreal, she has worked in the print industry as an art director, typesetter, and printing consultant. She entered the corporate world as a production manager for Delrina (acquired by Symantec), and has held senior marketing positions in global technology organizations, including Compaq (acquired by HP), DST Output,

BorderWare Technologies (acquired by WatchGuard), and Xenos, a division of Actuate.

Since 2011, Joanne has worked as an independent consultant, assisting B2B organizations with their lead generation and conversion strategies. She is currently the director of marketing for Avanti, a leading provider of Print MIS and Web-to-Print solutions.

Nikki Gore

Nikki is a veteran marketing executive with over twenty years' experience in the high-tech industry. Currently she is vice president of marketing at Infobright, where she leads product marketing and marketing communications. Previously she founded and ran Siren Marketing, a successful marketing consultancy. She has also held executive marketing positions at a number of large and mid-size companies, including vice president of marketing at QuickPlay Media, vice president of marketing at Critical Path, and senior marketing positions at Baan Company and Microsoft. Nikki completed the Executive Marketing Program for Technology Companies at the Richard Ivey School of Business and holds an Honours Bachelor of Arts degree from the University of Western Ontario.

Mike Hennessy

Mike Hennessy is currently the vice president of sales and marketing for Intelliresponse, a provider of digital self-service technology solutions. Mike has had a long and successful career as a technology marketer. He spent five years at Trution eCommerce (now Aptean Software) as vice president of marketing and alliances, where he led the corporate re-branding, partner development, lead generation, and market entry strategies for North America and Europe. Mike joined Intelliresponse in 2008, and spent two years as vice president of HE sales and marketing before becoming vice president of sales and marketing. He is responsible for demand generation, brand strategy, corporate messaging, advertising, public relations, and partnerships, and alliances. Mike earned his

MBA from Queen's University and a Post-Graduate Diploma in Marketing Communications from Seneca College. Mike holds two Deloitte Fast 50 – Fast 500 awards and has been published by MarketingProfs.com, CMO.com, Retail Touch Points, and ICMI.

Andrew Jenkins

Andrew Jenkins has provided social media strategy and social selling services to numerous large and mid-size enterprises over the past decade. His recent experiences include consulting to Royal Bank of Canada as head of social media strategy. He has spent the last twenty years working in information and communication technology (ICT) spanning social media, wireless, and e-business. He holds a BA in Economics from Laurentian University, a BFA in Film Production from York University, and an MBA from the Rotman School of Management at the University of Toronto. He also teaches entrepreneurship at OCAD University as well as Digital Strategy at University of Toronto's School of Continuing Studies.

Camille Kennedy

For the last five years, Camille has shaped the strategic marketing vision for Hip Digital Media, a company that specializes in promotional marketing technology by leveraging premium digital content rewards to drive brand sales. As the director of marketing, Camille is responsible for the development and execution of marketing initiatives, including managing outbound and inbound marketing tactics, such as email marketing, content creation, online and offline event hosting, social media, conference plans, and public relations activities. She also delivers strategic digital content solutions for Fortune 500 companies, including Kellogg's, Diageo, and Dr Pepper Snapple Group.

Camille began her career with Sony Music Entertainment in 2005 in the National Sales Division. There, she was responsible for managing customer marketing and promoting Sony Music products through Amazon.ca. She has completed a Master's Degree in Music Business Management from London's University of Westminster, and also holds a Bachelor of Commerce Degree (Honours) in Finance and Marketing from the University of Manitoba.

Colin McAlpin

Colin McAlpin has spent over seventeen years in software marketing for high-technology enterprises. He spent a number of years at Cognos, a business intelligence and performance management software developer. He joined in 1987, working in a number of progressively senior marketing roles from marketing specialist to marketing manager. Colin was also one of the original members of the Business Intelligence Product Division, the department that drove market leadership for Cognos. In 1993, he joined Fulcrum Technologies as the product marketing manager. In 1997, he rejoined Cognos as their director of market and business strategy before becoming vice president of applications, and later, vice president of business intelligence product marketing, where he developed go-to-market strategy and positioning for the franchise product line. Since 2005, he has been providing marketing and business strategy consulting and coaching services through Colin McAlpin Enterprises. Colin holds an MBA from the University of Ottawa.

Jennifer McGill-Canu

Jennifer McGill-Canu is a marketing and product innovation executive with over twenty years of experience helping global manufacturing firms grow and evolve. She is currently interim marketing director at SVP Worldwide Canada, the world's largest sewing machine company. Previously, she was corporate marketing director at Royal Building Products, a manufacturer and distributor of building materials, where she was part of the turnaround team, overseeing brand strategy and repositioning, new product development, and go-to-market strategy. As strategy and marketing director at Lafarge Gypsum in South Africa, she introduced strategic business planning to help grow the adoption of plasterboard in Sub-Saharan Africa. There, she was responsible for implementing marketing plans, new product introductions, and establishing a state-of-the-art training center for architects and building professionals. Jennifer spent three and a half years implementing global knowledge management for Lafarge in seventy-five countries worldwide. Her Canadian corporate experience includes roles of increasing responsibility at Royal Bank, McGraw-Hill Ryerson, and Grey Canada. Jennifer is active on a number of not-for-profit boards and holds an MBA from the Rotman School of Management at the University of Toronto.

Brian Mergelas

Dr. Brian Mergelas is currently the CEO of the Water Technology Acceleration Project (WaterTAP), a not-for-profit established by the province of Ontario and devoted to championing Ontario's water technology industry.

Following the completion of his PhD in Physics from Queen's University in 1995, Brian went on to design advanced pipeline inspection systems in the oil and gas sector. Noticing a gap in infrastructure funding in the municipal market, he went on to co-found the Pressure Pipe Inspection Company (PPIC), a firm involved in the development and application of pipeline inspection technologies. Afterwards, he briefly served as the senior VP of strategic and corporate development at Pure Technologies before joining WaterTAP in 2012.

An early proponent of content marketing and the importance of thought leadership, Brian has successfully commercialized a number of technologies in the global water sector. He is an active angel investor and serves on several boards, including the Ontario Clean Water Agency and the Children's Aid Foundation.

Ross Nepean

Ross is currently the VP of global marketing at TAB, a 700-employee, privately held records management company with operations in the US, Canada, and Europe. Following the completion of his MBA from Wilfred Laurier, Ross became director of international marketing and took over responsibility for lead generation and brand awareness for TAB's businesses in Canada, Europe, and Australia. An early adopter of content marketing strategies, he successfully repositioned TAB from a products company to a solutions company. Ross's expertise is in using a mix of inbound and outbound marketing strategies and tactics to capture strong and sustainable revenues. Ross has delivered presentations on inbound marketing best practices to the Canadian Marketing Association and MarketingSherpa.

Colleen Preisner

Colleen Preisner is the head of the marketing division of FCT (First Canadian Title), a wholly owned subsidiary of First American Financial. With over twenty years' experience in financial services marketing communication, she has developed a track record for using customer insight to drive meaningful and effective communications. Prior to joining FCT in 2010, she spent several years working on both the retail and wealth sides of several major Canadian Financial Institutions. More specifically, she spent nearly four years as the associate vice president of the TD Bank Financial Group. Prior to joining TD, she spent six years as the director of marketing and sales for the Royal Bank of Canada. Colleen holds a Bachelor of Business Administration from Western University.

Herb Saunders

Herb Saunders is the national managing director of American Appraisal Canada, a company that values tangible and intangible assets and provides advisory services to the businesses that own them. He works with clients in the public and private sectors to resolve issues in valuation, transaction and fixed asset management. Prior to joining the Canadian operations of American Appraisal in 1983, Herb worked with Great-West Life Insurance, Bank of Montreal, and a corporate finance boutique. Between 2004 and 2011, he worked in US operations managing the company's North American business development initiatives. During this period, he was also responsible for the company's global re-branding. Upon returning to Canadian operations, that latter experience, together with observable shifts in B2B buying behaviour, fostered Herb's strategic commitment to marketing at American Appraisal Canada. He earned a Bachelor of Arts degree at Trent University.

Pina Sciarra

Pina has over twenty years of global marketing and executive team leadership experience in the beverage and food industry. Most recently, as head of marketing and new ventures at ConAgra Foods, Pina was responsible for strengthening the company's strategies to drive more profitable growth and build stronger brand loyalty with retail partners and consumers. Prior to that, Pina was with The Coca-Cola Company for twelve years in various senior roles, leading businesses in Canada, the U.S., and Latin America. She began her career in brand marketing at Kraft Canada.

Today, her consulting practice is based in Toronto with a focus on professional services (B2B), retail, consumer products, and not-for-profits. She is a member of the National Advisory Board for the Salvation Army, where she leads a significant task team of retail industry experts in improving operations for their 300 thrift stores across Canada. Pina earned a BPE at McMaster University and an MBA from Queen's University.

Susan Smart

A seasoned B2B marketer, Susan has global experience working in start-ups as well as established organizations that have had to shift strategies to remain competitive. She has worked primarily in the financial services and technology sectors in leadership roles spanning marketing, communications, product marketing, and business strategy.

Currently she is director of marketing for Vena Solutions, a cloud-based corporate performance management company. Susan is responsible for overall brand and marketing strategy as well as public and analyst relations to enable the start-up to achieve aggressive growth targets in a highly competitive industry.

Susan holds certificates in Advanced Account Management from the Executive Education Centre of the Schulich School of Business, and in Business Design from the Rotman School of Business. She has a BA Honours in English and Psychology and a Master of Industrial Relations from Queen's University.

Elizabeth Williams

Elizabeth Williams has spent the past fifteen years developing and executing successful marketing plans for B2B organizations. Currently she is the director of marketing and communications at ADP, the world's largest provider of business outsourcing and human capital management solutions. Previously, she was the director of vertical marketing at Rogers Communications, where she built and led the vertical strategy and content marketing for the business segment. During her time there, she won the Rogers CEO award for her contributions to the LTE network launch and the Rogers Marketing Innovation Award for the "Celebrate Small Business" campaign.

Before joining Rogers, Elizabeth was the vice president of marketing at Marketrend Interactive, a leading provider of CRM technologies and marketing services to the North American automotive industry. Prior to that, she held a variety of positions in the insurance, technology, and financial services sectors. She contributes to the Canadian Marketing Association as a speaker, volunteer and guest blogger.

Dave Zavitz

As the senior vice president of sales and marketing at Canada Cartage, the largest provider of outsourced transportation fleet services in Canada, Dave Zavitz oversees corporate marketing and national business development. Prior to joining Canada Cartage, Dave ran the Generator Consulting Group, where he helped small and mid-size businesses develop and implement marketing and sales plans. Prior to this, Dave spent fifteen years with Livingston International, one of North America's largest customs and logistics services companies, where he held progressively senior roles in sales and marketing, culminating as vice president of sales and marketing.

Dave is a volunteer mentor for the Innovation Factory at McMaster University, where he provides leadership advice to start-ups by reviewing their business plans and evaluating their marketing strategies.

CHAPTER *Fourteen*

Introduction to the 20 Lessons

For B2B companies who want to put marketing to work, the twenty lessons are a guide book on how to make it happen.

The twenty leaders shared the stories of their careers, the lessons they've learned, the mistakes they've made, and the advice they feel is most important for both owners and leaders of mid-market B2B companies, as well as the marketers who want to help them grow.

I've captured their advice in twenty lessons, which span the elements of marketing, from planning to reporting. The lessons are full of pragmatic, hands-on tips and advice. All the lessons are based on practical experience rather than academic theory.

The lessons are grouped into six categories:

A. Start Here for Success

B. Guiding Principles of B2B Marketing

C. The First 100 Days

D. Working with Sales

E. Reporting and Metrics

F. Planning for Long Term Success

How to Read the Lessons

The lessons are written for both marketers and their bosses (CEOs and other business leaders). For consistency, I've written the lessons directly to the marketing leaders. For CEOs, that means when you're reading the lessons, put yourself in the shoes of your marketing leader and consider what implications the lesson has for how you support the marketing function in your business. You can also use the lessons to screen potential marketing leaders that you're considering bringing into your business.

A

START HERE
FOR SUCCESS

I start with these two lessons because success in B2B marketing often comes down to these two things:

Lesson One
Get Support from the Top

This is the first of the twenty lessons for a few reasons. It was the most common piece of advice the marketing leaders offered. Many of them said something like, "If there's only one thing I'd advise, it's this," or "If I could do one thing differently in my career, this is it." In addition, this lesson is also the first activity that marketing leaders undertake when they're evaluating a new role or assignment. Without this factor in place, they feel there isn't likelihood of success. And the final reason this is the first lesson is because it's not just important for marketers, it's essential for non-marketing leaders in any B2B company to understand.

Here's the lesson: in order for marketing to succeed, there needs to be support from the top of the organization. The ultimate leader in the business needs to be committed to what marketing can achieve for the company, and be committed to achieving those results – including getting over the challenges along the way (because there *will* be challenges). And this support needs to be <u>real</u>, not just lip service.

You may be thinking, "Yeah, of course there needs to be support from the top." Most people who've been in business for a while know that it's important to have support from the top no matter what the initiative is – it could just as easily be an operations, HR or IT program. But there seems to be a gap when it comes to marketing. Maybe it's because marketing is a new function for many B2B companies, so relatively few executives have a yard stick for what to expect. Whatever the reason, the experience of many B2B companies is that it can be easy to *want* to put marketing to work, but hard to stick with it when the going gets tough. And that leads to a poor outcome for everyone.

Here are four tools for securing and bolstering commitment for marketing at the top of any organization. If you're a marketing leader looking at an opportunity with a new company and you aren't sure if the leadership is committed, use these four tools to figure it out. If you're the CEO, think about these four areas and how you respond to them – you'll be able to gauge your real support for marketing based on your answers.

1.   Set a Marketing Budget

One of the primary ways to confirm the commitment of a company to marketing is to establish a marketing budget for the first year. This allows the head marketer to set expectations among the company's executive team, and gauge whether there's enough budget to achieve what the company says it wants to accomplish with marketing. If that commitment isn't there, experienced B2B marketers often won't accept a position with a company or take on a new project, since they know there's a high risk of failure.

Nothing gets a CEO's attention like a budget request. A committed budget for the first year is necessary for marketing to get off the ground and have enough runway to gain traction. How much budget is appropriate? That depends on many factors – I offer some suggestions in Lesson Twenty. But a commitment to a full year of marketing budget is a must for success in B2B marketing.

And since marketing's full benefits in B2B take more than a year to achieve, consider setting a framework for calculating the year two marketing budget as part of the initial request. (This is good to aim for, although it is often difficult to do when there is no data or track record on what results marketing can achieve).

Either way, it's critical to set and commit to a full year budget in order for B2B marketing to get off the ground.

2. Insist on Leadership Time for Marketing

Commitment isn't just about money. While the budget is an essential starting point, it's only half the battle. The other critical resource is time. One way for marketing leaders to confirm they'll get the time they need with the business leaders is to require a meeting every week with the CEO (or other champion) for the first three - four months of marketing.

> Marketing leaders and CEOs should *meet every week* in the first few months of implementing a marketing plan.

This is a smart way to ensure senior executives commit to making marketing work. It also demonstrates that the head of the business and the head of marketing are on the same page and can course-correct early when recalibration is needed. Making this kind of commitment clearly illustrates that the business leader is involved in making marketing successful. I've seen many marketing programs go off track and ultimately fail if the CEO didn't spend time with the marketing leader.

3. Have Marketing on the Executive Committee

The support of the CEO is vital for marketing success, but on its own it isn't always enough, especially in larger businesses where there are other senior leaders (C-suite and SVP/VP roles). In these cases, the support from the CEO needs to be accompanied by support from other senior executives. If there is an executive committee responsible for major business decisions and strategy, it's important that the head of marketing be on that committee and have a voice during strategic planning and decision making. Without that, the marketer will be seen as just a function head without any real credibility or influence among those who drive the business.

4.   Have the CEO "Own" Major Marketing Initiatives Internally

The last tool to help secure support for marketing from the top is to have the business leader take responsibility for championing marketing internally. Employees within the company, from senior to junior, need to see that the head of the company is behind marketing and is personally involved. There are many ways that business leaders can demonstrate this. The CEO can present the marketing plan to the company at a company-wide meeting (a town hall) or through a company newsletter or conference call, or can be the speaker in the company's first webinar. Whatever the tactic, the business leader needs to be an internal champion of marketing to show the whole company that marketing is a strategic function and has the attention and commitment of the leadership.

The Lesson in Practice

The marketing leaders I interviewed had both success stories and disappointments when it came to having support from the top.

Take Dave Zavitz's experience. Dave joined Canada Cartage as SVP of sales and marketing in late 2012. He had previously run a growth consultancy for mid-market companies, where he had advised Canada Cartage, working directly with the company's president. After several months as an advisor, Dave was asked to join Canada Cartage full time. Because of his previous working relationship with Canada Cartage's president, Jeff Lindsay, Dave was able to gauge his level of commitment to marketing. Dave knew that Jeff understood marketing's value, and when Dave asked for commitment to a first year marketing budget, Jeff made it. Jeff also participated in all the initial marketing planning workshops alongside the company's senior executive team – clear commitment of their time and attention.

And on the other hand, there are disappointments when support at the top isn't there. As a cautionary tale, one marketing leader shared his experience as head of marketing for a large company (several billion in revenue) in a mature industry. He had been brought in to help the organization become the dominant brand in the industry. When he was interviewing for the role with the company, he had some concerns that the CEO didn't truly understand what value marketing could bring to the business. Acting on those concerns, he put several of the four tools to use – he confirmed a first year budget and had the CEO own several important initiatives internally. He thought this was enough to ensure that there was true support rather than pretense for marketing. He wasn't able to secure a place on the executive committee though, and that ended up being the issue. In his first few months with the company he interviewed other senior executives and learned that one of the two SVPs was categorically opposed to marketing. In fact, at their first meeting the SVP stated he would not support marketing in any way. And he was true to his word.

The marketing head navigated the turbulent waters for a couple of years. He was successful in streamlining the company's product lines, launching a brand overhaul, and updating the company's digital and physical presence. But ultimately the lack of real support for marketing at the senior level prevailed and the marketer was out of a job within two years, replaced by product managers at a divisional level, in roles that were at best tactical marketing, certainly not strategic. In our conversations, the marketing leader expressed no surprise that this had happened and chalked it up to a lack of support at the top. It's a mistake he won't make in future.

Nikki Gore, the vice president of marketing at Infobright, shared a good tip on how she evaluates whether there's commitment from business leaders to a strategic marketing leader (as opposed to a marketing "order taker"). She's had conversations in her career with business leaders in which they've stated categorically, "We already know what our problem is – we just need someone to come in and fix it." She considers this a hazard flag. Unless the B2B company has

RED FLAG:

"We already know what our problem is – we just need someone to come in and fix it."

had a high-performing marketer in the past, it's unlikely they know exactly what to expect from marketing and how to make it happen.

Putting the Lesson into Use – A Caveat

As I mentioned earlier, the caveat for putting this lesson to use is that relatively few B2B executives have had experience with marketing. As a result, they have limited experience in what level of commitment is appropriate and what benefits strategic marketing will deliver for the company. When I asked the marketing leaders about how their company leaders had acquired a strong belief in marketing and an ability to make a commitment to it, many of them said that they'd had positive exposure to marketing in previous roles. Either they had been in B2C companies and entered B2B, bringing with them an understanding of the value of marketing, or they had previously worked in B2B companies with successful marketing functions.

This can make support for marketing at the top a chicken-and-egg scenario: the executives have never experienced effective marketing, so they can't make a significant commitment to it. And if they don't make a significant commitment to it, it can mean they won't be successful in marketing.

But there's good news on the horizon. First, I see more and more B2B company executives making a commitment to marketing based on the encouragement of their boards of directors and advisors, or through observing the success of competitors' marketing, or by witnessing other mid-market B2B companies' growth through effective marketing. And second, I see a greater number of experienced B2B marketers (although still not enough) who know how to put a plan in place that will deliver incremental wins and grow the success of marketing quarter by quarter. These two factors means that while strategic marketing is still a new function for many B2B companies, there is a growing willingness to commit to it.

Lesson Two
SET REALISTIC EXPECTATIONS

One of the main challenges for any executive when they start to implement a strategic marketing process in their business is to build marketing capacity, including a shared understanding of what marketing is, what it can be, and what it is not. In many B2B companies, non-marketing executives have a strong background in sales but are limited in marketing. So there's an inevitable learning curve to identify what marketing can accomplish and how long it takes. Like so many things in life, it always looks simpler, easier, and faster than it actually is. I often compare marketing to building a house or doing renovations – before I'd done any home renovations, I thought, "How hard can it be – just take out this wall, put a new one over there, slap on some new paint and we're done!" The actual experience of renovating taught me a lot, and how much more goes on behind the walls that can't be ignored.

So the second lesson is this: establish realistic expectations. Of course, if you're a CEO who has never done any marketing, your response will be, "How can I have expectations when we've never done this stuff before?" A reasonable qu___n, which I'll hopefully answer here.

If the expectations of a B2B company are for revenue results from marketing in a three-month horizon, it can be very difficult for marketing to deliver. This is true for digital marketing and traditional marketing tools. Although digital advertising, like pay-per-click (PPC), can generate quick results, it's usually only when there's a solid marketing platform in place – a marketing strategy, a website that clearly articulates the company's value proposition, and excellent content.

Digital advertising can generate quick results only when there's a solid marketing platform in place – a strategy, a clear value proposition, and good collateral and content.

In addition, the speed with which marketing can generate revenues is affected by other variables that are unique to each company, like the length of the purchasing cycle. In complex sectors where purchasing is a long process with many stakeholders, it's unlikely that marketing can deliver radical results in a short time. There is a Warren Buffett quote that I think captures the reality of the pace of B2B marketing well, "No matter how great the talent or efforts, some things just take time. You can't produce a baby in a month by making nine women pregnant."[23] And that's exactly it – in B2B, some things just take time.

Business leaders should be wary of short timelines for marketing. It's better to have both *quick-win goals* and *long-term strategic objectives*.

---

23   http://onforb.es/1ydf1C6

For marketers starting new leadership roles in B2B companies, it's important that the companies' goals are achievable. There are ways to help set and manage expectations, but if the starting point is for revenue results in a short timespan, it can be an irreconcilable situation. Both non-marketing and marketing leaders should be wary of short timelines for marketing. A better approach is a balance of short timelines for some marketing deliverables with longer horizons for lead and revenue results.

All business executives will naturally ask, "When will we achieve results from our marketing?" And in response, marketing leaders should ask a few questions of their own. Here's a shortlist of questions to help set realistic goals for marketing:

1. What is the purchasing process and timeline for the products/services we sell?

2. How many people are involved in the decision to purchase what we're selling? Is it typically a large group or a single person?

3. What's our marketing gap? Do we have a good strategy and market awareness but haven't pursued new business (a lead generation gap), or do we have a non-existent reputation and are selling against large, well-respected competitors (a market awareness/credibility gap)?

4. What is the current level of marketing? Are we starting from a standstill or has there been a robust marketing function previously?

5. What's the current state of the pipeline?

The answers to these questions help marketers set realistic timelines. And while every situation is different, most marketing leaders agree that it takes three to six months to build the marketing founda-

It takes 6 – 12 *months* to see consistent pipeline growth in most B2B companies.

tion and get marketing underway, six to twelve months to see consistent pipeline growth, six to eighteen months for consistent revenue growth, and two to three years to build a tightly calibrated marketing machine that delivers measurable results. In Lesson Sixteen, I share additional details on realistic timelines for marketing. These parameters are averages, and every company's situation will be different. Brian Mergelas, who now runs WaterTAP, shared the story of the longest purchasing cycle he's witnessed; ten years to secure a deal for a water infrastructure project in the Middle East. Thankfully, not all B2B companies face such long purchase horizons, but twelve to eighteen months is hardly uncommon. Executives should keep those timelines top of mind when they're looking for quick results from marketing.

That leaves marketers with the challenge of setting realistic expectations for the specific situation they're in. To help with that, here's a prototypical case from one of the companies I've worked with recently, a services company with revenues under $5 million that had done minimal marketing in the past.

The first year of data shows the pre-marketing activities. There were some big spikes in revenue, which gave the business owner misgivings since the company would have big deals one month, and then drop back down to very little business. The lack of consistency was frustrating for the business leader.

Marketing started in October of 2012. But as the data shows – it didn't make much of a difference in the first six months. In fact, things appeared to get worse – with no deals at all in January and February 2013. Those were stressful times for the owner – he was making the investment in marketing, but the results weren't showing. His commitment to the long-term success of marketing was essential to getting through that rough patch. And by the twelve-month mark, things were clearly improving – not only the revenues, but the consistency of the revenues. From there, they've only increased. That's how marketing works – with a good plan, a good execution team, and commitment to see things through, by the one year milestone, marketing should be consistently performing and delivering, and performance over years two onward should continue to improve.

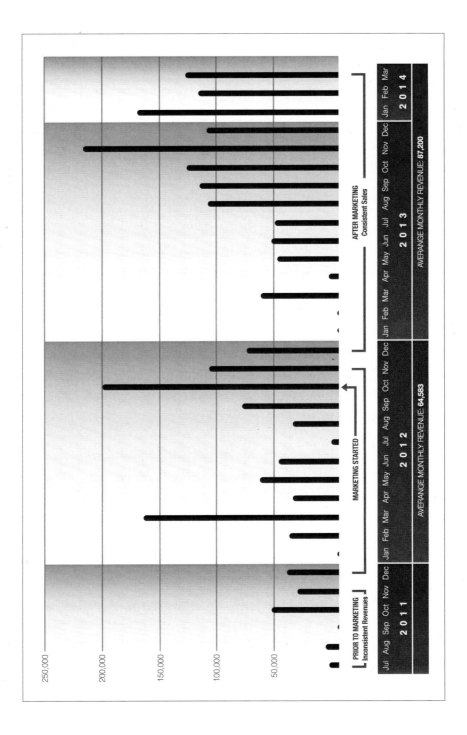

There is an upside when it comes to managing expectations of marketing in a B2B environment. As Colleen Preisner, director of marketing at FCT, which provides title insurance and other real estate-related services to lenders, legal professionals and real estate professionals noted, "When a B2B marketer joins an organization that doesn't have a lot of experience with marketing, it can be easy to find the quick wins that will demonstrate immediate business impact. For example, launching a website that presents a strong strategy and begins to immediately drive traffic and leads will get plenty of attention. The most important thing is for marketers to choose their early tactics wisely — so they can demonstrate the tangible impact of marketing."

Herb Saunders, the head of American Appraisal Canada, took a realistic approach to setting goals for marketing. His company values the tangible and intangible assets used in primary and secondary industries and intangible assets like intellectual property rights for companies in the digital space. The company operates in a sophisticated market and has traditionally relied on the efforts of its principals and business development officers to bring in new business. But seeing a slow but steady decline in the efficacy of that approach, Herb embarked on a program to put strategic marketing to work for American Appraisal Canada.

His long-term horizon and commitment to marketing was three years; he knew that it would take more than a year to see the benefits that marketing could bring because of the long buying cycle in his industry. He undertook an initial planning process and then began implementation. And while his horizon was long term, he also had short-term milestones. When the implementation didn't go as he initially expected, he made changes to personnel within four months. From there, things have been on track, with small revenue wins in the first year, and growing success in year two. For companies operating in complex and mature industries, where there has been limited marketing in the past, a two+ year time-horizon is a smart way to go.

And while marketers often have to manage unrealistic short-term expectations, they also must keep in mind the longer-term vision and capabilities of marketing. When Dawn Abankwah joined Spafinder as the VP of business development to head up the company's gift card sales expansion in Canada, she laid out a five-year vision for marketing and what she wanted to accomplish. As Dawn said, "To be a truly strategic function within a business, marketing needs to guide and support the long-term view of where the company can go."

> Marketers need to deliver results in their *first year* in order to prove marketing's worth and ensure there will be a budget for a second year.

Dawn's approach to managing short and long-term expectations of marketing at Spafinder was to establish a five-year vision, and then work backwards to set goals for year one, and then by quarter. She knows that marketers need to deliver results in their first year in order for marketing to secure continued investment. This is critical in B2B companies. Because marketing is new for many B2Bs, there is a risk around year one that the program will be defunded. That's a waste, as marketing has strong potential to be a strategic function for B2B companies.

One final point about setting realistic expectations. I've seen a number of cases where companies think that marketing can solve fundamental business ills, like product reliability issues or customer service problems. Marketers refer to this as the "lipstick on a pig" approach. Marketing absolutely cannot solve these problems.

Companies should always solve their fundamental issues before they embark on marketing, to avoid making product or service problems worse and causing a lack of credibility. In B2B, word spreads quickly, so companies who plan to embark on marketing should ensure they have a solid foundation. Marketing works best when a company is very good at what it does, but is not that great at getting the word out.

B

GUIDING PRINCIPLES OF B2B MARKETING

There are six major tenets to B2B marketing success:

Lesson Three
DON'T BE THE ART DEPARTMENT

When I asked Dave Zavitz what had been important for him to do in his early days as SVP of sales and marketing at Canada Cartage, his answer was both hilarious and brilliant. He said, "I needed to demonstrate to everyone that marketing was not about choosing a new colour for the logo. In short, I needed to show everyone that marketing isn't the art department."

> *Strategic marketing* is about increasing awareness, generating leads, and increasing loyalty among customers. It isn't about the colour of the logo.

This lesson is so vital for B2B marketing success that it's number one in this next section of lessons, the six big tenets of B2B marketing. B2B marketers need to be ever-mindful that B2B companies often have not had a lot of experience with marketing. In many cases, they don't know what marketing is. But they often think they know what marketing is – and the common perception is that marketing is something to do with the colour of the logo and the golf balls the company gives away at its annual golf tournament. B2B companies often have somebody in-house who has created their brochures and catalogs in the past. That person has often carried the title of marketer, but those activities are actually graphic design. Strategic marketing is about establishing an effective position for the company in the market, increasing awareness of the company, generating qualified leads, and increasing loyalty and share of wallet among existing customers.

Elizabeth Williams of ADP shared the story of how she learned to correct misperceptions of marketing early in her career. She agrees that B2B marketers need to work hard to not be seen as the art department. One of the tools she uses to establish a more accurate understanding of marketing is a calculator. She always brings one with her to meetings, and although she doesn't always use it, having it there and occasionally using it to run numbers completely alters the perception of those around her – both marketers and non-marketers. Her peers quickly realize that she is numbers-driven and that marketing is about the financial results it delivers for the business. This is a simple and effective tip for B2B marketers. They need to be serious about the numbers, and just as importantly, they need to be seen as serious about the numbers in order to battle the perception of marketing as the art department.

Leslie Carter, the chief brand and strategy officer at Knightsbridge, and previously the chief marketing officer, echoed this sentiment. When she started as CMO at Knightsbridge, there was no marketing department. Without an established strategic marketing function, many of her colleagues didn't understand her role. As a result, she found that she received many requests to create brochures or perform some other graphic design task. In order to ensure the marketing team wasn't perceived as the art department, Leslie established a specific vendor (graphic designer) to be responsible for collateral and design tasks. Leslie has seen many instances in her career where junior marketers, in the name of being helpful, do absolutely anything that is asked of them – including brochure design and presentation preparation. They quickly become seen as graphic designers. And that's bad for the strategic marketing function, and for those marketers' careers. It is too easy for marketing to become a graphic design department if marketers don't establish themselves as focused on delivering revenues. B2B marketers need to be vigilant to eliminate every perception of marketing as "art."

In an ironic twist, the lack of resources that most B2B marketers face is helpful for correcting this misperception about marketing. As Christina DiLallo at Newcomp shared, B2B marketers can almost always point to a limited budget as the basis for not taking on non-strategic and non-revenue-generating initiatives. If marketers are to deliver on the strategic aspects of their role, they cannot take on all of the tactical and operational requests that come their way – especially when those tasks have more to do with art than science. This is a great tip because it allows marketers to share their strategic focus with colleagues through both words and action – and while it can take a few months for the message to get through, eventually the non-marketers realize that their marketing team is not the company's art department. And that's good news for the business – it means faster growth because the marketing is focused on revenue and profit generation.

Lesson Four
HAVE THE RIGHT ATTITUDE

There are so many things in life that require the right attitude. The challenge for most people isn't that they have a bad attitude, it's that they don't know what the right attitude is. This is particularly true for aspiring B2B marketers, because there are relatively few mentors and academic programs for B2B marketing. To complicate matters, the marketing field is dominated by consumer marketers – and a consumer marketing attitude can be disastrous in a B2B environment if it isn't carefully adjusted for the different constraints and success factors.

Here are four tips on the "right" attitude for mid-market B2B marketing:

1. Take Responsibility for Revenue Generation

It used to be that marketing and sales were completely separate entities. Historically, in most mid-market B2B companies, marketing's role was generally as the servant of sales – marketers would produce the collateral the sales team asked for. At best, the marketing function was responsible for lead generation, and would hand over leads to the sales team who would be solely responsible for securing revenue. Unfortunately, this dynamic created the mindset that marketing is a support function that is not directly linked to, or responsible for, generating revenue.

As I discussed throughout Parts One and Two, marketing and revenue generation are no longer separate. Without a marketing function that understands it has a responsibility for revenue generation at the early stages of the purchasing process, and stays involved to ensure leads

effectively to paying customers, B2B marketing is not fulfilling and B2B companies suffer declining revenue.

.lity for marketing:

OLD REALITY

NEW REALITY

Great B2B marketers today have a revenue generation attitude. They understand that their role involves collaborating with the sales team to ensure successful revenue generation.

B2B marketers must take real ownership for **revenue generation**. They have to think that revenue generation is absolutely their responsibility, not the job of the sales department.

Mike Hennessy of Intelliresponse put it this way, "B2B marketers must take real ownership for revenue generation. They have to think that revenue generation is absolutely their responsibility, not the job of the sales department. It's the job of the marketing and sales departments. If it's not the marketer's mandate, then someone else will definitely pick it up and run with it, effectively reducing marketing's ability to provide measurable value that matters. The minute that a marketer says, "revenue generation is the responsibility of the sales department" is the minute they've lost their job."

Colin McAlpin shared a good quick tip on how he internally "checks in" on whether a strong revenue generation attitude exists within the marketing department. He asks himself, "How many people in the marketing department are thinking about revenue on a daily or weekly basis?" If the answer isn't everyone, he knows he has some work to do. It's a simple tool, but effective. If he feels that the marketing team is waning in their revenue generation focus – something he can evaluate based on what the team is talking about and planning – he knows he has to recalibrate the focus of the team.

2. Expect to Roll Up Your Sleeves

The reality in B2B marketing is that you will never have all the resources you want or need, which means you have to get your hands dirty. Jennifer McGill-Canu shared the story of how she single-handedly got social media underway at Royal Building Products. Even though she was in charge of a multimillion dollar marketing budget, she did the company's tweets herself. Why? Because while she knew social media would be an effective tactic for Royal over the long term, she didn't have any data to show her peers and therefore, she couldn't build a business case to get budget for social media. So, for a full eighteen months, she ran the social media efforts for Royal herself and, in doing so, she showed an incredible "roll up the sleeves" attitude that I think is a great example to other B2B marketers.

The other element of rolling up your sleeves for B2B marketers is that they're often teaching themselves how to do new things. WordPress – sign me up! Pinterest, let me at it! A new webinar software – I'll figure it out on the weekend! For marketing leaders, it's not a question of signing up for a course that their boss has suggested they might want to take – it's about cobbling together a working knowledge of new technology before anyone else has even thought to offer a course on it. The pace of change in marketing is so rapid now that training courses and seminars can't keep up. So marketers who don't want to be a year or two behind take the initiative to constantly figure out new things. They don't think twice about working extra hours to investigate a new tool or find data for a particular initiative they're thinking about launching. Having a passion for learning and taking the initiative to pursue them is critical to success in B2B marketing.

3.   Be Resourceful

Every B2B marketer experiences limited budgets on a regular basis. In B2B it's a given. But the good news is that the most creative solutions come from these limited budgets. Successful B2B marketers have learned the power of being creative when it comes to how they achieve their marketing plans. Whether it's repurposing content, doing contra deals, or finding a contractor at a great rate, B2B marketers are always resourceful and innovative in accomplishing their goals.

4.   It's Good to Give Away Expertise

There's a new attitude required for success in the era of the New Buyer, and it's an attitude that doesn't always come easily for executives who operate in traditionally competitive B2B markets. The attitude is one of sharing expertise – widely and freely.

Because the New Buyer completes more than half of the buying process before engaging with sales, she gains a significant amount of knowledge about a potential purchase. B2B companies who feel they need to closely guard their knowledge miss out on demonstrating to potential buyers that they have a lot of relevant expertise, and often the deal entirely.

For professional services companies, whose expertise is primarily what they sell, or industrial companies who face fierce competition, the notion of sharing expertise can be controversial. But it's the most effective way to raise awareness and establish a position as a thought leader.

Speaking about her role as marketing advisor for a law firm, Pina Sciarra recounted the importance of sharing the firm's expertise as the starting point for conversations with potential clients. If the firm hadn't been willing to share its knowledge without charging a fee, there would have been relatively few opportunities for strategic marketing.

For professional services companies, whose expertise is what they sell, the notion of giving away expertise "for free" is counter-intuitive. But it's the best way to establish a position as a *thought leader.*

One of the approaches that Pina has seen work well is executive seminars, where lawyers share expertise and recent experiences with company owners and managers as a way of teaching them what's on the horizon. As Pina says, "B2B companies now have to first demonstrate the value they can provide. They have to show it, not just tell it. Only when they've first done that, do they get the opportunity to charge a customer for their expertise."

GOOD MARKETING
STARTS WITH BUSINESS ACUMEN

This lesson builds on a theme that runs through the previous lessons – that strategic marketing is often misunderstood in B2B companies, and smart marketers have to correct misconceptions in order to achieve the potential of marketing.

Great B2B marketers all have a similar approach to marketing. They don't think of marketing as the goal in and of itself. They think of marketing as a tool for achieving business objectives. Put another way, great B2B marketers are business thinkers first and marketing thinkers second. This is clear in many of the things they do – from striving to establish marketing as a strategic function (rather than an art department) to their diligent focus on revenue generation. It's this orientation that makes a great marketer a strategic asset for a B2B company.

To do this, B2B marketers need to fundamentally understand how a business makes money. As Camille Kennedy explained, marketers figure out the margins in their various products and services, which channels are the right fit for their target market and which types of marketing will drive ROI. And once they have that understanding, they make investment decisions based on how marketing will best fulfill the business objectives.

Great B2B marketers are business thinkers first and marketing thinkers second.

This is the crucial difference between a good B2B marketer and a great B2B marketer. There are many good B2B marketers. Marketers who know how to develop brands and collateral, how to create and distribute content, how to implement marketing automation technology, and how to create and execute a social media strategy. But all of those skills are tactical. To add strategic value for their organizations and earn a seat on the executive committee, B2B marketers need to understand how to increase revenue and profit for the business. When marketers can do those things, as well as manage operational and tactical marketing plans, they become strategic business leaders and vital members of the CEO's team.

Developing these skills takes time. Sometimes academic programs like an MBA can be helpful. But only a third of the marketing leaders I interviewed have MBAs. The others had all successfully developed their business acumen through their careers, and had the good fortune to work with other marketers or business leaders who helped them gain their business acumen and apply it.

Business acumen helps marketers in almost every facet of B2B marketing, from developing the marketing strategy, to allocating the budget, to effective score carding and reporting. But first among these facets is defining the marketing strategy. As Herb Saunders, head of American Appraisal Canada advised, marketing's first role in any business is to ensure that the marketing strategy is sound, that the company is differentiated in the market, and that there is a clear value proposition that resonates with customers. If a marketer is not able to determine these things, all of the other tactics they implement will not add up to profit.

The importance of business acumen is one place where the difference between B2B and B2C marketing is especially clear. In consumer marketing, a creative idea can often generate tremendous returns. Business acumen is important in consumer marketing, and that power is matched by the power and importance of creativity. In B2B marketing, the tables are turned. Strategy and execution are the drivers of success. Creativity is nice to have in B2B marketing, but not a necessity. Just look at the prevalence of creative directors to understand the difference. Creative directors are a large constituency in B2C marketing, but

I've yet to meet a creative director in B2B marketing. Of course, it's wonderful to have B2B marketers who have creative skills, but if I had to choose between business acumen and creative skills in a B2B marketer, I'd choose business acumen every time.

Many of the revenue generation leaders agree with Susan Smart, director of marketing for Vena Solutions, who says that all B2B marketers in the future will be well-rounded. "B2B marketers in the future will focus on the hard side of the business, not just the soft side. They'll understand customers and structure effective messaging for them, but they'll also understand the financial underpinnings of the business, know how to use data and be able to measure effectiveness."

Lesson Six
KNOW YOUR TARGET MARKET

Everyone knows the rule that you can't be all things to all people. This is especially true in B2B, where transactions tend to be high value and customers expect a high level of customization and specialization for their exact needs. There is tremendous power in focusing on a specific target market, which enables companies to tailor messaging and content for distinct types of customers (market segments) based on their industry, job function, geography, or other meaningful variables. But homing in on a specific type of customer is easier said than done, especially for companies at an early stage of growth. It's more comfortable to pursue any kind of customer at all than to narrow the focus to a smaller group of potential customers. But focusing on a niche or segment of the market is the key to achieving exponential growth. This lesson is about how to home in on your specific market.

Defining target segments can be done a few ways. Some companies have sufficient internal data to generate a strong market segmentation. That was Dawn Abankwah's experience when she was running the B2B gift card program at HBC. The company had a large customer base and substantial transaction data, which was essential to understanding the market segments and identifying which customers were more profitable and should be pursued, and which should not. Through her market segmentation process, Dawn uncovered compelling insights about the profitability of different kinds of customers. To the surprise of many of her colleagues, the customers that were the highest volume purchasers were also the least profitable, and one category of buyers who were lower volume buyers were in fact the most profitable. These were the customers that HBC wanted to capture! Accordingly, they were the customers that Dawn selected as a high-priority target market.

Having access to that data enabled Dawn to identify where the profits really were. By understanding the different segments and their relative value for the business, Dawn was able to tailor programs and marketing communications that would attract and grow the best kinds of customers, which led to a very successful marketing function.

It's rare though for a B2B company to have a treasure trove of internal data. The reality for most B2B businesses, especially small and mid-sized enterprises, is that there is a limited customer base and relatively limited transaction data. And looking externally isn't much help either, as it's expensive to conduct customized market studies. The practical approach for creating a market segmentation is to leverage the experience of the sales team to identify different types of customers, and pinpoint those that are the best fit for the company.

> The marketing team can leverage the experience of the sales team to identify different *types of customers*, and pinpoint those that are the most profitable for the company.

Companies who clearly define their target customers have much more effective marketing. One of the important tools that B2B marketers use to illustrate and focus on a target maret is the persona. A persona reminds the sales and marketing teams about who the buyer is and why they need you. Here are seven questions to create a target customer persona.

1.   What kind of organization does the individual work in? What industry? What size of company?

2.   What is their title/role? What are they typically responsible for?

3.   What is their current situation? What problems are they trying to solve?

4.   Is there a typical process they follow to find solutions to their problems?

5. What decision criteria do they have for working with new vendors?

6. Are they savvy about solutions to their problems, or do they need to be educated?

7. Are they early adopters of technology or laggards?

And here's an example persona:

EXAMPLE INITIAL PROSPECT PROFILE:
Validation Consultant/Validation Engineer

Profile	
	Status: Working, between the ages of 40-65.
	Gender: 8:2 ratio of males to females.
	Key Characteristics: Conservative, will not take chances when making purchasing decisions.

Buying Behaviour	
	Process: Will conduct validation research on latest news and explore investment options.
	Information Sources: Prefer product information emailed to them or presented to them at industry events.
	Active in industry forums and webinars and attends tradeshows.
	Budget: Influences budget, but does not have control of budget or final say.
	Key Decision Criteria: Security, accuracy, risk avoidance, documentation and integration with current IT processes.

While most B2B companies can identify up to a dozen different types of customers, it's necessary to narrow the focus to about three personas. This is important because most B2B companies don't have the resources to execute marketing for more than three segments (large companies with more resources can handle more). In Lesson Eight, I share a framework for prioritizing target markets.

When developing a target market persona, keep in mind that B2B purchases typically involve multiple decision makers. There are often different functions and levels of seniority involved in a particular purchase. This impacts the marketing program, as different tactics and messages are needed to address different stakeholders. For example, Leslie Carter at Knightsbridge commented on how buying behavior for human capital solutions is completely different between senior executives and junior employees. While a junior staff member may be asked by a supervisor to identify options for a particular talent development issue, the decision making will happen at the senior level. But both people (and others) are involved in the purchase process. As a result, the marketing strategy and tactics need to address the needs of both the senior and junior buyers. Thought leadership and the company website are important tactics to get on the radar of the junior person when he's looking for solutions, but activities like networking and speaking engagements are important to raise awareness and achieve credibility in the eyes of the senior decision maker. B2B marketers typically develop personas for the different individuals involved in the purchase decision so that they can develop marketing materials that speak to the different individuals involved in purchasing what they sell.

> B2B purchases involve multiple decision makers. *Good marketing* will speak to all the important stakeholders.

One facet of segmentation that is receiving a growing level of attention is personalization. The need and ability for B2B companies to refine their communications based on prospects' individual preferences is increasing. Marketing automation programs are now adept at serving up content based on a prospect's most recent interaction with a company and their level of engagement. For example, if a prospect downloads a white paper from the website, they will likely receive a follow up email or voicemail. For prospects who respond to that email or voicemail, the nurturing process will continue through additional offers of content. Those that do not respond will receive an alternative offer at some point in the coming week. Marketing automation technology is powerful for companies who have the resources to make it work. It isn't for everyone though. I've seen many companies invest in the technology and then not have someone to operate it, which is like buying an expensive golf club and then never having any time to play golf.

One last suggestion – Camille Kennedy provided a great tip on segmentation. Whenever her company closes a new deal, her team looks at the prospect database to identify other companies with a similar profile (i.e. in the same segment). They then promote their new deal to those companies to demonstrate what the similar company achieved. It's always important for marketers and business developers to help prospects connect the dots on how a company's solutions can help them solve the particular issues they face.

Whether the marketers define the target market using internal data, external research, or a combination of the two, the key takeaway is that it's powerful to focus marketing resources on specific segments of the market. B2B companies have to focus their marketing efforts where they'll get the best returns, and knowing their target market helps them do that.

Lesson Seven
BE HEARD FROM ALL DIRECTIONS

We all deal with information overload. The average person in North America is exposed to at least 5,000 brand messages a day, and some estimate the number to be as high as 30,000 a day.[24]

> Contacts between a buyer and a seller are called *touch points*.
>
> A touch point can be in digital or tangible format – anything from an advertisement to an email to a mention in a trade publication article or a meeting at an industry conference.

Because of that volume, it takes a lot more for any single message to get through. The old marketer's rule of thumb was that a message had to be heard between five and seven times in order for it to be remembered. Now, most marketers feel we need somewhere between eleven and thirteen touches before a message "breaks through." In some cases, particularly in complex B2B sectors, the number is even higher.

Knowing the number of touch points needed to get through to a buyer is important for B2B revenue generation. It helps marketers and sales people plan their programs and set realistic expectations for the timing of results. For example, Janet Campbell at TAB uses a ten to sixteen touch rule. She knows that between the marketing and the sales teams' efforts, a prospect needs to hear the TAB message between ten and sixteen times before a deal will be done. Janet, who runs the TAB's sales function, and her marketing counterpart, Ross Nepean, use that ten to sixteen touch framework to structure TAB's marketing and sales process and tactics. Their

24   http://linkd.in/1pFfzWN

combined efforts have to achieve that range of touches, in the right manner and at the right time, to maximize success.

Every company has a different number of appropriate touches based on its industry and target market. And every company has lucky situations where a customer is in the right place and time, and a deal can be done with just a few touches. But in general, it now takes more than half a dozen touches, coming across multiple channels, for prospects to even know of a particular company – let alone do business with it.

We now need somewhere between *eleven and thirteen touches* before a message 'breaks through'. In some cases, particularly complex B2B sectors, the number is even higher.

Many companies are still adapting to this new "noisy" reality that their buyers live in. Buyers consume many kinds of media – from their LinkedIn update feed to trade publications to mainstream business media. As Lori Wizdo at research firm Forrester said, "Without debate, the business *from* business buyer is already much more multichannel than business-to-business sellers are. Buyers of business products and services are online, in social channels, on YouTube, going to events, and evaluating options on their iPads and smartphones."[25] B2B marketers have to cover a lot of channels to keep up with buyers.

This complexity is difficult to manage, because with the limited resources they typically have, it's tough for B2B companies to deliver multiple messages through multiple channels. This is where it's critical to have a clear target market (Lesson Six) and a solid understanding of the most important stakeholders in the purchase decision. Since the vast majority of B2B purchases involve a growing number of stakeholders at different levels of seniority and with different functional responsibilities, B2B companies with limited resources need to have a laser focus on the right buyers in the process and know which channels will get their message through to those buyers.

---

25   http://bit.ly/1tUNKQs

Touch points are valuable because they accelerate the sales process — or at the very least, they accelerate how the purchasing process is *perceived* by the seller. If more than half of the buying process is complete before a buyer engages with a salesperson, it's essential to use marketing to generate as many touches as possible during that "invisible" phase, since marketing is almost always a lower cost way to achieve touches. A company that has effective marketing will have touched a customer several times before it even knows the name of that customer. Indeed, the goal of marketing is to move the customer as far along the buying process as possible, so that the sales team's time will be well utilized when they do connect with a buyer.

There's a caveat to this rule though. B2B companies need to use a few different channels to get a company's message in front of a buyer multiple times, but they also need to be realistic about their resources. I've seen many companies plan too many initiatives across too many channels and not have sufficient resources to effectively execute them. Companies that are new to marketing shouldn't take on any more than three to five communications tactics. As they gain experience and put processes in place to manage the different tactics, they can then take on more.

Lesson Eight
BE A RESOURCE ALLOCATION WIZARD

As I've mentioned in several lessons, if there's any guarantee in B2B marketing, it's that there will be limited resources. And this reality gives rise to many of the behaviours that make for a successful B2B marketer, including this lesson about being a resource allocation wizard.

Each of the marketing leaders shared stories about how they had stretched budgets, created successful campaigns out of zero dollars, found vendors who could deliver what they needed on a shoestring, and other heroic tales. In talking with them, I realized that a limited budget wasn't something they complained about or lamented. If anything, it was a challenge and badge of honor for them to make results happen where others would have wilted. And that's an indicator of the kind of marketer who thrives in B2B – those who take pride in what they can accomplish under constraints.

The challenge of limited budgets is most prevalent in mid-market B2B companies where marketing is a new function. I've seen many companies where there isn't a line item or area of the P&L for marketing – meaning there's been no budget for marketing in the past. When the starting point is zero, it's a long way to go to get to a reasonable budget.

But great marketers deal with this by being resource allocation wizards. They're great at figuring out what marketing to do and when. Because there's an awful lot to do to get marketing working in a B2B company, a strategy needs to be developed, collateral and content must be created, marketing tools have to be implemented, and campaigns and marketing tactics need to be run. Elizabeth Williams of ADP put it this way, "To run a full B2B marketing program with limited resources means you need to be very strategic and creative. You have to cover off multiple target markets, multiple decision makers involved in a purchase, and multiple touch points across multiple channels. The complexity is significant."

Here's how great B2B marketers make decisions about where their limited resources will be allocated:

1.   Prioritizing Target Markets

While it's challenging for companies to narrow their focus to one or two priority markets, they're almost always more successful by doing so (Lesson Six). There are two primary variables that help prioritize target markets:

   a.   Where does the company currently have the greatest traction (customer base or experience)?

   b.   Which market has the greatest opportunity?

And of those two variables, the first is the most important by a wide margin. Unless there is a compelling reason not to pursue a market where a company already has traction (for example, a regulatory or economic change that will cause the decline of the market), then it's the best place to start. In B2B, a track record is essential, and companies who have success in a particular niche or industry are looked upon favorably by potential clients in that niche – which means marketing can deliver results quicker.

2.   Prioritizing Decision Makers

There are usually multiple decision makers in a B2B purchase, although it can vary based on the chosen target market. When it comes to prioritizing decision stakeholders, use these two variables as a guide:

a. Who is the most senior person involved in the decision in a chosen target market?

b. How difficult is it to get to that most senior person?

Anyone responsible for revenue generation wants to deal with the economic decision maker – the person who has the ability to make the financial commitment to the purchase. But often that's not possible – and the larger the organization, the more difficult it can be. So marketers should pursue the highest level they can, but must be realistic that some of their tactics will need to target less senior decision makers in order to ensure they're getting on the radar.

3. Prioritizing Aspects of Marketing

As I outlined earlier, there are five elements of marketing for B2B companies:

1. Developing a marketing strategy – identifying the value proposition, target markets, and positioning.

2. Raising awareness of the company – ensuring that prospects know about and think positively of the company.

3. Generating and nurturing leads – attracting potential customers so that the sales team has the opportunity to engage with qualified potential buyers.

4. Supporting the sales team – ensuring the sales team has the tools and collateral to be effective in discussions with target customers.

5. Increasing retention and share of wallet - educating the existing customer base about the company's breadth of services and applications so that they do a growing amount of profitable business with the company each year.

These five factors are the chain of marketing, and as with every chain, marketing is only as strong as its weakest link. Great B2B marketers identify the greatest weakness in the company's existing marketing and address it first. Where is the key pain point in their organization's marketing? Does the company have a market awareness problem? A lead generation problem? A strategy problem? There's no point in raising awareness if the company has a credibility problem, or in generating leads if the company's sales support is broken. Smart marketers allocate resources to the marketing area that needs the most attention, and then they repeat the process in order to get all five areas working in relative balance.

4.   Prioritizing Tools, Tactics, and Campaigns

And finally, B2B marketers have to be savvy about what they're going to tackle and when, recognizing that they need to show immediate results and also position marketing for long-term success. Often, they need to keep the long-term horizon in mind, and balance that with short-term outcomes that generate cash flow. This is where prioritizing gets hard. While the brand might be important in the long term, the investments required in order to develop and launch a new one are significant. While the corporate identity is important, it's not more important than lead generation in the short term – because that will get positive results and more revenue in order to tackle the corporate brand issue later on.

Susan Smart of Vena Solutions agrees about prioritizing revenue generation in the short-term: "Anything that makes an impact on revenue – whether it's helping out with an RFP or creating a one-pager that will progress a conversation on a particular deal. In the short term, B2B marketers need to show that they are focused on revenue generation, not academic concepts like brand building."

When it comes to prioritizing tools and tactics, B2B marketers have to resist what I call "shiny marketing syndrome." It can be difficult to say no to new ideas and opportunities, but B2B marketers have to be strict in their resource allocation – if they pick up a new marketing initiative, they likely need to drop another. Usually it's the non-marketing executives who make this challenging – there can be many "flavor of the month" marketing ideas.

And the last tip about resource allocation is something that B2B marketers learn early in their careers – the importance of leveraging resources for multiple purposes. As Joanne Gore shared, "You need to repurpose your marketing assets. For example, your case study becomes a press release and pitch, which becomes a webinar, which becomes a white paper – again and again." Joanne shared an example of how she repurposed a number of webinars when she was at Xenos, a division of Actuate. After developing a webinar for a very technical audience, she used it as the basis for a webinar aimed at a business audience. She knew that she needed to cover off both the business and technical stakeholders involved in a typical purchase decision, and the benefit of using the same webinar base for both audiences was that there was some consistency and crossover. The stakeholders could relate to each other's perspectives, and it took Joanne only a fraction of the time to produce the second webinar from existing material rather than starting from scratch.

To recap, the six key tenets of B2B marketing are:

1. Don't be the Art Department
2. Have the Right Attitude
3. Good Marketing Starts with Business Acumen
4. Know Your Target Market
5. Be Heard From All Directions
6. Be a Resource Allocation Wizard

In the next section, I'll discuss how leaders put these tenets into practice, specifically in the first 100 days of marketing.

C

THE FIRST 100 DAYS

Great B2B marketers pack a significant punch in their first 100 days on the job. Here's how they do it:

Lesson Nine
DELIVER QUICK WINS

Lesson Two covered the need for realistic expectations, and that means both the long-term and the short term horizons. Lesson Nine is about delivering quick wins — how marketing leaders produce tangible and visible accomplishments as quickly as possible. This is a critical step in building credibility and trust in B2B marketing, which lays the groundwork for greater success down the road.

Use a "First 100 Days" approach for delivering quick wins.

Many of the twenty leaders use a "First 100 Days" approach for delivering quick wins. Many spoke about the need to get specific things accomplished in that timeframe in order to set the marketing function up for success and leverage the energy and excitement the company has for marketing in this "honeymoon" phase. Even though the business leader has made a long term commitment to marketing (Lesson One), marketing leaders need to build confidence across the organization in order to win over skeptics and validate the decision to invest in marketing.

Mike Hennessy set and accomplished several goals in his first 100 days with Intelliresponse. He identified new target markets, developed a new brand identity and messaging, overhauled the company's web presence, and created a new sales structure. He also had a white paper and webinar produced. That's a phenomenal output. Not every company will be able to absorb that amount of marketing drive or activity in the first 100 days, but some will — and the more the company can accomplish in those first few months of marketing, the better the results will be every month after that.

Every company has a different set of activities that make the most sense and deliver the most value in the early stages of marketing. There are no set recipes, but here are some activities to consider:

- Marketing Strategy
- Brand Update (not necessarily an overhaul – often a refresh will do)
- Website Overhaul (including keyword strategy)
- Collateral Update
- Sales Process Definition

The list above includes a number of activities. Some of the activities produce tangible results – like a new website or new collateral. Others produce results that are less tangible but no less important – like a new strategy. The challenge for the B2B marketer is to accomplish both foundation activities, like confirming a strategy, as well as tangible outputs, like collateral, in order to be seen as delivering quick wins.

Leslie Carter also took a quick wins approach when she joined Knightsbridge. In her first three months, she created a brand strategy for the company and then had the strategy tested and refined. This enabled her to get agreement on the strategy and move on to implementing it in the following months.

At Canada Cartage, Dave Zavitz's approach was to demonstrate traction in the marketing function and deliver tangible results for the sales team in the first 100 days. He took a two-pronged approach. First, he outsourced the majority of the marketing function to ensure he could quickly access a diversity of marketing skills and resources and get a plan built quickly, and a team executing that plan within the first 100 days. At the same time, he knew that the sales team would be more enthusiastic if they could see specific outputs, which meant leads. Accordingly, Dave also launched an outbound lead generation program that would deliver qualified leads for the sales team.

Every company will have a different set of activities that makes the most sense as quick wins. It's the marketing leader's job to determine which results will be seen as quick wins, and to then determine which tactics are best to fulfill those objectives. Here are some options to consider (not an exhaustive list):

1. **Marketing Strategy**
   Target markets, value proposition, positioning

2. **Messaging**

3. **Content Development**
   Articles, blog posts, white papers, infographics, ebooks, podcasts, videos

4. **Collateral**
   Company overview, brochures, sell sheets, case studies, video

5. **Events**
   Webinars, trade shows, seminars, conferences, customer appreciation events

6. **Cold Calling/Telemarketing**

7. **Database/CRM**
   Clean up or implementation

8. **Email Marketing**

9. **List Development/Segmentation**

10. **Advertising**
    Digital, print, radio, outdoor

11. **Website and Search Engine Optimization Strategy**

12. **Social Media**
    LinkedIn, Twitter, Google+, Facebook

Lesson Ten
PICK THE RIGHT BATTLES
AND COMMUNICATE THEM

I think every chief marketing officer, VP of marketing, or marketing director feels the same when they take on a new role. There's a sense of excitement about the possibilities and opportunities ahead, and there's also a sense of anxiety about managing the expectations of their new colleagues and navigating the path to success. As I discussed in Lesson Two, the expectations of marketing in B2B companies can sometimes be aggressive, if not simply unrealistic. While smart marketers do their homework before taking on a new role to ensure there aren't impossible expectations, there's still the real challenge of managing expectations.

Marketers have the most ability to manage those expectations in the first 100 days. Because of this, marketing leaders take a proactive approach to not only selecting their priorities, but even more importantly – communicating them. And communicating them again. And again.

Once a marketing head has reviewed the numerous options for allocating their limited resources, they make decisions about the marketing priorities in terms of target markets, buyers, facets of marketing, and tactics. Putting that plan together is a major accomplishment. But it's only half of the planning task. The other half is equally important.

The second half is <u>communicating</u> the plan and restating it frequently so that there's clarity on the priorities, why they're the priorities, and what the outcomes will be. This process is critical to ensuring clarity on what will be delivered by marketing, and when, so that the team is aligned in its expectations.

Colin McAlpin shared his method for ensuring he picked the right battles and declared his intentions. When starting with a new team or division, he interviewed the members of the sales group. Through this process, he heard about the countless priorities each person had for marketing. In conversation with each person, he posed questions that helped not only him, but also his colleagues, evaluate where the true priorities lay. It was an effective way to gain buy-in prior to setting out and presenting his plan. When he ultimately presented the plan, there were no surprises for the team on where the priorities were. Colin needed only to continually communicate the plan and deliverables to achieve a shared understanding of the marketing function.

Many of the marketing leaders mentioned that the sales team often wants marketing to pursue new customers. New customers are often seen as the sexier, more exciting goal for marketing initiatives. But the twenty leaders had all experienced better, faster returns from pursuing *existing* customers rather than new customers. In most cases, marketing should resist the temptation to pursue new business at the launch of a marketing function. If the company has done very little in the way of communicating with past and current customers, there is often a significant opportunity for fast results by focusing there.

The best way to pick battles and declare your intentions is to treat your internal stakeholders (non-marketing executives) as a target market. If you have a clear understanding of how to communicate with that market and how many touch points are needed to have your message get through, and then execute your plan, you'll be successful.

And finally, Colleen Preisner has some sage – if tough - advice. One of the best ways to demonstrate intentions is by making changes to the existing marketing team. If there are members of the team who don't have a revenue focus and the ability to deliver results, the marketing leader sends a powerful message by removing them from the team. It demonstrates a focus on achieving results and that tough changes will be made to get there.

Lesson Eleven
GET ALIGNED ON GOALS

Sales executives typically describe marketers as "academics" and "irrelevant." Marketers often describe sales people as "cowboys" and "incompetent." *This will have to change*.

This last lesson about the "First 100 Days" approach focuses on aligning goals within the company, specifically between sales and marketing, where there can be friction in B2B companies. In a recent CEB survey,[26] sales executives typically described marketers as "paper pushers," "academics," and "irrelevant." Marketers, meanwhile, described their sales counterparts as "simple minded," "cowboys," and "incompetent." A full 87% of the terms used by either the sales or marketing team to describe the other team were negative.

This will have to change. As the buyer continues to take more control of the purchasing process, a disconnect between the sales and marketing teams will cost B2B companies more each year. And conversely, organizations who have good alignment between sales and marketing will reap even greater returns and be tough-to-beat competitors.

Andrew Jenkins, chief strategist at Volterra Consulting and an instructor of digital strategy at the University of Toronto, shared an experience that reveals the profound problems that arise when sales and marketing aren't aligned on goals. Earlier in his career, he worked at a major Canadian telecommunications company that had hundreds of sales people and marketers across the country.

---

26   http://bit.ly/1odatlC

The sales and marketing teams had a dysfunctional relationship that frequently caused problems. The underlying issue, and something that no amount of communications or coaching could address, was that the sales team was compensated on top-line revenue while the marketing team was compensated on profitability. That might not sound like a big difference, but from a business objectives standpoint, it's cataclysmic. In essence, the sales team would pursue all new revenue, even if it was low or negatively profitable, while the marketing team would only want revenue that came with high profits – so they would oppose many revenue opportunities. In short, a good sale for the sales team was often a bad deal for the marketing team, and vice versa. Because top line revenue and profitability are often opposing goals, there was no way to get alignment between the sales and marketing teams.

Andrew's example reveals a structural problem that prevented sales and marketing from working effectively together. Fortunately, situations where there's a direct conflict between the sales goal and the marketing goal is, in my experience, relatively rare. Based on what I've seen and what the marketing leaders shared, it's far more common for there to be no <u>obvious</u> conflict or disconnect between the sales and marketing teams – because there's simply no clarity on what their individual or shared goals are!

> The sales team was compensated on *top-line revenue* while the marketing team was compensated on *profitability*. No amount of communication can solve that.

That seems shocking at first blush, but every marketing leader shared stories about the challenges of achieving clear goals between sales and marketing. The reality is that it isn't a quick or easy process. Mike Hennessy at Intelliresponse explained that it takes expertise, committed sales and marketing leaders, and ongoing effort. In his experience, it can take two to three years to build a tightly engineered sales and marketing collaboration in which there are clear goals and interactions between the two teams. And that's for companies who have relatively well-structured sales operations. Since the vast majority of B2B mid-market companies don't have developed sales systems and processes it can take even longer to achieve goal clarity between the sales and marketing teams. But it is vitally important, and the marketing leaders shared good tips on how to accomplish it. Here are their top five tips on how to get sales and marketing working as an efficient team:

1. Don't Aim for Perfect, Just Start

Getting sales and marketing in perfect sync is a long-term goal that can't be resolved immediately. As Joanne Gore advised, "Don't aim for perfect accuracy when you start working on sales and marketing alignment. You'll have to make assumptions and estimates at first – but unless you start tracking, you won't have any data in order to refine your estimates and get accurate forecasts." Don't be afraid of being wrong the first year, because you will be. Being right isn't what matters – starting the process is.

2. Start by Establishing the Revenue Goal

The first step in aligning sales and marketing is to be clear about the revenue or profit goal for the company. This number can comprise different types of deals – for example, both new and existing customers. Setting a reasonable goal is vital in order to get the commitment of the team that will deliver on it. The goal should be based on past years' growth and the relative investment in growth – for example a company that is making no investment in sales and marketing shouldn't expect to double in size unless some other external factor (like regulatory change) is driving that growth.

3.   Delineate the Sales Process

Many companies haven't delineated their sales process into stages such as introduction, needs assessment, demo, that map to the buying process. Companies should define their selling process. Keep the pinball pipeline in mind – the traditional funnel is not always a good depiction of how buyers move from one stage to the next, but there are certainly stages that buyers go through on their journey to a purchase.

4.   Figure Out the Revenue Generation Math

With a revenue goal established and a delineated sales process, companies can use a few simple questions to work backwards to determine the number of deals they need at various stages of the selling process to achieve the revenue goal.

1. What is the revenue goal?

2. What is the average deal size?

3. Divide the revenue goal by the average deal size to determine how many deals are needed.

4. What is the conversion rate from lead to deal?

    *   Many companies don't have actual data on this, and that's okay. Use estimates based on experience as a starting point, and then put a process in place to track deals and get actual data over a six – eighteen month time horizon.

5. Divide the deals needed (#3) by the conversion rate to determine how many qualified leads are needed to meet the revenue goal.

Here's an example:

Revenue goal: **$1,000,000**

Average deal size: **$20,000**

Deals needed: **50**

Conversion rate: **25%**

Leads needed **200**

If the answers vary significantly from deal to deal, multiple sales process structures might be needed. This is often the case if, for example, a company does a lot of deals with existing customers and the conversion rates for existing customers are different than those for new customers.

5.   Implement a Closed-Loop Process

Sales and marketing need to clarify the definition of a qualified lead.

Now the real work between sales and marketing begins. There should be regular communication between sales and marketing about the pipeline and what's working and what isn't. Establishing the framework allows the sales and marketing leaders to draw some lines in the sand on the business goals and determine the respective goals of sales and marketing. They need to keep the first step in mind – that it isn't about being perfect or even being right, it's about working towards better results.

The sales and marketing leaders should work closely together – which I'll talk more about in the next two lessons – over the course of a year in order to gain clarity on how lead generation and the sales process really works. This is all part of the process of building an effective revenue generation machine.

One of the key areas that sales and marketing need to clarify is the definition of a *qualified lead*. That's the most common disagreement between the teams – marketing feels they provide a good volume of leads, and sales feels like marketing feeds them too many unqualified leads that aren't worth their time.

WORKING
WITH SALES

In the last lesson, we looked at how sales and marketing teams can get aligned on the shared revenue generation goal, starting within the "First 100 Days". In this section, we'll look at more ways sales and marketing can work together effectively.

Lesson Twelve
SUCCESS STARTS AT THE TOP

There's a growing argument that the sales and marketing functions in B2B companies will disappear as separate entities and evolve into a "revenue generation" team with roles that correspond to the new buyer behaviour and purchase process. I believe we'll see that occur in more B2B companies over the next five years. The process has begun in some companies who have chief revenue officers.

Today, though, most companies are still accustomed to the concept of a sales team and a marketing team. And there are ways to ensure these two teams work together well to achieve successful revenue generation. The most important element is that a good working relationship between the sales function and the marketing function starts at the top. It starts when the leader of marketing and the leader of sales – if they are different people – make conscious efforts to work in an integrated way. It starts with the attitude that revenue generation is the shared goal of sales and marketing.

Smart sales leaders tend to know that a great marketing leader will make their job easier. They know that with good marketing, the sales team will have qualified leads to pursue and they'll need to do less of the tough work to generate leads. They also know that a revenue-focused marketing leader will take some of the pressure off the leader of sales, because the heads of the two functions will share the responsibility.

Here are four ways B2B marketing leaders establish good working relationships with sales leaders:

1.   Understand the Sales Leader's Mindset

When Andrew Jenkins begins work with a new organization, his goal is to build an effective working relationship with the sales leader from day one. To achieve this, he holds meetings, preferably informal ones, before he does anything else. As he says, "What the org chart tells you and what actual people tell you are two entirely different things. I find a relaxed conversation over coffee yields incredibly powerful insight on what matters to each individual and how they think. That helps me identify how to create an effective working relationship." He then outlines his framework and approach to marketing, what he expects to accomplish in his role, what he expects to deliver for the sales leader, and how he suggests they work together to achieve the company's revenue goals. This gives comfort and confidence to sales leaders because it demonstrates to them that his focus is on delivering revenue results and that he will hold himself accountable for them. Many of the marketing leaders spoke of a similar approach in which they build relationships and share their direction in order to gain confidence among their peers.

2.   Create Shared Definitions

One of Ross Nepean and Janet Campbell's first objectives in working together at TAB was to define a qualified lead and continue to evolve it as they gained experience. Earlier in his career, Ross had seen situations where leads had been accepted by the sales team, but were not in fact qualified. That led to the sales team blaming marketing for not understanding and focusing on the right goal – revenue generation. In fact, it had been an issue of poor collaboration between the sales and marketing teams. Ross learned that having clarity on the definition of a qualified lead was the key to success.

Start with a definition of a qualified lead and evolve it over time.

The definition of a qualified lead is one of the most important topics that sales and marketing leaders can work on together. It's amazing how much of a difference there can be in the perspectives. Joanne Gore humorously described what happens if the sales and marketing leaders don't work together on a valid definition, "The marketing team will define a lead as a heartbeat, while the sales team defines it as a done deal." With such varied interpretations, nothing less than frequent, honest discussion between the heads of sales and marketing will resolve it.

3.   Try Things Out

Nikki Gore's advice for making a collaborative environment between sales and marketing is to be responsive and open whenever the sales organization brings ideas to the marketing team, especially in the early stages of the relationship. "If sales people come to you with an idea that you think won't ultimately work, but it's feasible from a financial perspective, try it anyway. The sales team will be more open to working with you in future and if it works, great. Even if it doesn't, it's the opportunity to collaborate on something and will make the sales people more open to your opinion in the future."

4.   Be the Head of Sales *and* Marketing

What about when the head of sales and the head of marketing are the same person, as is the case for anyone who carries the title of VP of sales and marketing (or a variation of it)? In my experience, that is a powerhouse role for revenue generation when the individual has a strong background in marketing and appreciates the role that marketing can fulfill in the age of the New Buyer. Often though, because of the traditional sales dominance within B2B companies, there are sales leaders who've been given the title of marketing in addition to their sales title, but in fact they have limited experience and interest in the function. If they have a vision for the impact that strategic marketing can have on the company's revenue generation efforts and can find a good marketer to work with, they'll be successful. If not, it doesn't tend to deliver incremental results for the company.

Lesson Thirteen
COMMUNICATION MECHANISMS

Almost all B2B marketers are good communicators when it comes to customers. What differentiates good B2B marketers from great ones is that great marketers are also excellent communicators when it comes to their internal audience – the sales team. Here are six tools and methods for communicating effectively with the sales team.

1.   Weekly Meetings

Weekly meetings ensure that the sales and marketing teams are talking frequently, paying regular attention to the integration of the revenue generation activities, and evaluating the effectiveness of various initiatives.

Typical sales and marketing meetings are sixty to ninety minutes. When establishing the working rhythm between sales and marketing, a ninety-minute meeting is often needed to start. Don't rush the meeting in the first month or two – you can scale back once you've created an effective meeting structure and pace. Some companies separate information-update meetings (weekly) from results-review meetings (weekly or monthly), depending on the size of their sales and marketing teams. This usually happens when companies grow to a point that it doesn't make sense to have as many people attend the results-review meetings.

Start with a weekly 90-minute meeting to establish a working rhythm between sales and marketing. Scale back once you've created an effective meeting structure and pace.

Different companies will have a different rhythm of leads and business, so some sales and marketing teams have bi-weekly sales meetings rather than weekly. Either is fine. However, monthly meetings between sales and marketing are not effective – the time gap between meetings is too long and people fail to get into a habit of good, structured communication.

Camille Kennedy at Hip Digital Media holds weekly sales meetings to review the marketing calendar and to ensure sales and marketing are aligned. In the meeting, she presents what marketing has planned for the month ahead so that sales can align their activities around major events like trade shows and webinars. Camille also reviews the marketing qualified leads at the weekly meeting so that there's a frequent feedback loop for marketing on what's working and what needs to be adjusted in terms of scoring the leads passed over to sales.

2.   Training Sessions and Memos

Dave Zavitz uses another tool for communicating marketing activities to the sales team. He shares the overall marketing plan with the sales team at the start of every fiscal period, and whenever a new tactic is being launched, he adds a training session or memo to explain what the tactic is, why it is being used, and how it will go to market.

For example, when Canada Cartage launched its customer newsletter, Dave provided a detailed description for the sales organization about who was receiving the newsletter, what the purpose of it was, and when it was being sent out. It's important that sales know what marketing is doing (and vice versa), and this additional tool is a good example of the adage that you can never communicate too much.

3.   Have Marketing Go on Sales Calls

One of the best ways to help marketers understand customers and what a salesperson's job entails is to have marketers attend sales calls. While the logistics can be tricky, the effort pays off a thousand-fold. Whenever I attend a client's sales calls, I almost always get a huge "aha." It's an immediate way to see into the world of the customer and understand their issues and what the sales team needs to do to educate and convert them. Having marketers join sales calls almost always builds understanding between the sales and marketing teams, and makes the marketers better at what they do because they have a deeper understanding of customers – all those things add up to radically improved effectiveness of marketing and sales.

4.   Use Data

One of the most important tools for effective communication between marketing and sales is to use data as the platform for discussion. As Dawn Abankwah says, "Data never lies. Both the sales and marketing leaders need to have confidence in the data and understand the nuances of what's going on behind the data, so that they can use it to have productive discussions about what's working in sales and marketing."

Using data ensures that anecdotal evidence doesn't get taken as fact. In the absence of robust data, a single bad lead from a particular source can be extrapolated into a bad marketing campaign. Which is often untrue – there isn't enough data to reach that conclusion. If a campaign generated

Use data to ensure that anecdotal evidence doesn't get taken as fact.

ten leads, all of which were unqualified, then it's reasonable to conclude the campaign isn't effective. Data should be the basis of communication between sales and marketing whenever possible.

5. Sit Together

Mark Fasken of Influitive has seen many sales and marketing teams through his career both in business development and in consulting on sales effectiveness to B2B companies. He suggests that one of the best, and simplest, ways to ensure that the two teams work well together is to have them sit together, or at least in close proximity. If adjacent rooms or spaces are available at the company's office, having sales and marketing sitting alongside one another enables the teams to build relationships – both casual and formal – that help the teams work together, and it also gives the marketing team the opportunity to overhear the phone conversations that sales has with customers, which is invaluable in helping marketing understand customers' reactions to marketing messages and key pain points.

6. Don't Stop at the Leaders

Lesson Twelve focused on the relationship between the sales and marketing leaders because a weak relationship there will often doom the two teams from working well together. But close working ties shouldn't stop at the leaders – they should extend throughout the sales and marketing teams. Even if there aren't many people on the teams, find ways to structure interaction between marketers and sales people, and have them directly address any operational issues that arise (rather than elevating them for the heads of sales and marketing to address).

Lesson Fourteen
HOW TO STRUCTURE INSIDE SALES

A recent study in **Harvard Business Review** showed that more than twice as many companies are shifting towards inside sales than are adopting outside or traditional sales forces (46% choosing inside sales vs 21% for outside sales).

There is a growing role for inside sales in B2B companies. As the study in the note above states, more companies are shifting to inside sales than the other way around.[27]

This trend is especially strong in mature industries where products can be commoditized and margins are tight. These companies benefit from an inside sales model for several reasons:

- **Reach** – Inside sales can cover more customers and geography through their efforts than an outside rep can.

- **Effective Transaction Support** – With so many customers completing part of their purchase process before contacting the sales team, in many cases there is no sales process to be undertaken – simply a transaction to be processed. Inside sales is more efficient for this.

- **Outbound Focus** – Companies often attempt to get their outside sales reps to do cold calling or lead generation activities to no avail. Somehow, other activities always seem to fill up the calendar of the outside sales team! But with an inside sales team, specific members of

---

27   http://bit.ly/1e1OPka

the team can be dedicated to outbound calling and lead generation, so there's no excuse for the calls not to occur.

- **Sustainable Cost** – Inside sales reps are typically paid 40% – 60% of outside sales reps, and spend much less on travel and entertainment expenses, so they're better positioned to help B2B companies achieve a sustainable cost of sales, which is critical in increasingly margin-tight B2B industries.

Inside sales reps are typically paid **40% – 60%** of outside sales reps, and spend much less on travel, so they're better positioned to help B2B companies achieve a sustainable cost of sales.

Inside sales is the right model for a growing number of B2B companies. There are several approaches on how to structure an inside sales team and which tasks to assign to inside sales. There's no right or wrong model, simply models that are more or less appropriate in a given environment. Here are a few ways that B2B companies use inside sales as part of their revenue generation team:

1. **LEAD GENERATION** – The inside sales team is solely focused on outbound efforts (email and calling) to generate qualified leads for the outside sales team. They may produce their own lists or receive them from another team. Often they are measured by the number of meetings they set up for the outside sales reps, and how well those meetings convert into opportunities.

2. **ACCOUNT MANAGEMENT** – Inside sales reps "farm" an existing portfolio of clients and ensure that relationships with existing customers are maintained and upsell and cross sales opportunities are identified. These inside reps are often measured on the revenue increase achieved within their customer base.

3. **SALES SUPPORT** – Inside sales reps support outside reps and remove administrative tasks from them. They often conduct research and prepare presentations and proposals. This is stretching the concept of inside

sales, as this structure is more accurately focused on administration rather than revenue generation. But the intent is to optimize the time of the outside sales reps, and it can be a good way to train future potential sales people.

4. TERRITORY MANAGEMENT – Inside and outside reps partner to maximize the revenue from a territory from both new and existing customers. Inside sales handles existing customers and screens incoming opportunities, and hands more complex opportunities over to the outside rep. This is similar to account management – the difference is that in this model the team handles both new opportunities and existing customers in a particular geographic region.

5. TRANSACTION – If the product or service that the company provides is straightforward, the inside sales team can be responsible for efficiently transacting simple deals.

With the increasing complexity of B2B sales, it's less common and effective for a single rep to take a buyer through an entire purchasing process. By focusing inside and outside sales team members on specific steps in the sales process (for example generating leads, farming the existing client base, or supporting an outside sales team member), the overall team becomes far more efficient. However, not every company can afford multiple people for their inside teams. In those situations, it makes good sense to look for a high-quality contractor or outsourcing firm.

One concern with inside sales is whether the team should be managed by the head of sales or the head of marketing. At Intelliresponse, inside sales is responsible for lead generation and qualification, so the team reports to the head of marketing, Mike Hennessy. In other inside sales models – for example the account management structure, where there is a focus on generating revenue from the existing client base, inside sales is usually managed by the sales leader. Mark Fasken suggested that the most important characteristic in the reporting structure is that inside sales (and any sales reps) need to be managed by those who have experience in the sales function. Without in-depth understanding of the nuances of the sales process, even the best manager will struggle to help their team succeed. So a marketing manager who has a background in sales will be a very effective manager for an inside sales team, while a marketer who has spent their career in content marketing won't be.

There isn't a right or wrong reporting structure. The quick rule is that if the inside sales team is primarily focused on farming and supporting customers, then it reports to sales. If it is primarily responsible for new customer acquisition, then it reports to marketing.

While many of the marketing leaders had positive experiences with inside sales reps, not all found that it was the right structure for their business. For instance, inside sales was not the right solution for Pressure Pipe Inspection Company (PPIC). Brian Mergelas found that, given the complexity of the solution that PPIC provided and the difficulty of finding buyers and influencers, inside salespeople simply didn't have the level of expertise to be able to connect meaningfully with customers. So in PPIC's case, experienced sales reps were the only way to go.

One final point to keep in mind, any company that has both an inside and an outside sales force must have a CRM (Customer Relationship Management system – like Salesforce.com, Dynamics, Sugar, Zoho, or one of the many others) in place. A CRM is necessary to facilitate the tracking and coordination of which prospects and customers have been touched, by whom, and when.

Lesson Fifteen
BALANCE SALES AND MARKETING

The last lesson in this section on working effectively with sales focuses on the balance that is necessary between the two functions. For many mid-market companies, marketing is a new function that introduces new people and processes, which requires integrating new marketing activities with existing sales activities. A certain amount of calibration (in addition to lots of collaboration) needs to happen between the two functions to achieve success.

There are three facets to balancing the sales and marketing functions:

1.　Balancing the Marketing Image

Have you ever gone on holiday or to a restaurant that had amazing imagery and reviews on their website, only to find that the reality was vastly different? I think we've all had those disappointments. And we end up thinking far less of the business because of that disconnect between the expectations they set and their reality. It's no different in B2B. Sure, marketing needs to present a certain image of a company in order to attract the attention of customers (most B2B companies want to look bigger and more advanced than they are – marketing is about growth after all), but if the image portrayed is significantly different than reality, customers will only be disappointed. They not only won't do business with the company, they'll avoid it in the future and tell others to do so as well. B2B marketers therefore need to strike a balance between what the company is today and what it wants to be. Because if the sales, operations, customer service and other functions of the business are dramatically different than how marketing portrays them, customers' expectations will not be met. And that's worse than doing no marketing at all.

2.   Balance the Marketing and Sales Activities

This section could also be called "Balance <u>and Clarify</u> the Marketing and Sales Activities," since both balance and clarity are critical for success between the two teams.

Figuring out which revenue generation activities are sales and which are marketing can be a complicated affair. There's no single right way to structure the responsibilities, and most companies have a different set-up. The most important element is clarity. When everyone on the sales and marketing teams is clear on who's accountable for what, they're able to focus and get the right things done.

Here's a list of activities that are commonly performed by marketing or sales (usually with the input of the other team):

MARKETING	SALES

Marketing Strategy

- Market research, including competitive intelligence, market sizing and segmentation, and customer intelligence.
- Definition of target markets and positioning.

Product Management and Strategy

- Guidance on new product development and road maps based on market research.
- Product launch strategy and execution.

Content Development and Dissemination

Market Awareness

- Can include PR, social media, advertising, trade shows, seminars, and other events.

Lead Generation and Nurturing

- Campaign development, deployment and measurement.
- Can include list development and outbound lead generation, such as telemarketing or emailing, webinars, direct mail, and email marketing.
- Lead nurturing for prospects who are not yet ready to buy.

Sales Strategy

Networking

- Attending events where customers and partners are likely to be

Inside Sales

- Account or territory management model (see Lesson 14)
- Transaction processing

Qualifying Prospects, Conducting Detailed Needs Assessment

- Working with qualified prospects to understand their specific needs and tailoring the company's solution to them

Solution Development and Proposal Preparation

- Customization of solution and pricing for individual customers

Prospect Meetings and Presentations

- Attending in-person, telephone and web meetings with clients to assess needs and present options

- Can include 'inside sales' if the team is focused on new customer acquisition rather than organic growth.

Sales Support

- Development of collateral and tools that support the sales team.

Customer Retention and Growth

- Upsell, cross sell, and other communications to increase share of wallet and retention of customers.

Marketing Measurement and Reporting

Account Management

- Managing and growing a book of business over time

Partner/Channel Management

- Training, coaching and performance management of distributors or agents

Revenue Forecasting

- Preparing and sharing quarterly (or other timeframe) sales forecasts for the operations and finance teams

Sales Measurement and Reporting

3.   Balancing the Sales Team's Skills

Because the New Buyer is better informed and further along the purchasing process than in the past, the first interaction she has with the sales team is a major milestone and potential pivot point. If the sales team member that she deals with is knowledgeable and able to deliver useful information, a productive conversation takes place – which usually leads to another conversation along the buying process. However, if that first conversation isn't useful – or on par with competitors – the buyer will drop that supplier and move on to the next.

One of the big changes with the advent of the New Buyer is that salespeople need to be expert calibrators. Buyers are all at different stages of the buying process when they contact sales – some are in the early stages of their process and others may be practically ready to buy.

To quickly establish a relationship with a potential buyer, salespeople have to be able to calibrate to each customer's stage of the buying process at the moment that they call or email. Does the customer already understand their problem and the options for solving it? Do they understand the pricing of the various solutions? Or is the buyer at the start of their due diligence and calling the salesperson as a sort of informational interview? Good salespeople will ask a few questions and listen to the responses. And based on what they hear, they'll pick up the conversation at exactly the right point for the customer. It's this skill that often differentiates a junior sales person from a senior salesperson, and is often the difference between no deal and a great deal.

> A salesperson's ability to calibrate to the *buyer's level of knowledge* is the biggest differentiator between a junior salesperson and a senior salesperson.

The lesson is that B2B companies need a balance of senior and junior sales skills in order to effectively deliver sales given the complexity of what the company sells, and to deliver those sales cost-effectively. Sometimes B2B companies make the honest error of hiring a junior salesperson with the plan that they will train them up in their environment. On the surface, there's nothing wrong with this plan. But unfortunately, with a lot of B2B companies the training of a new salesperson never happens. In this scenario, even very talented junior salespeople are rendered ineffective. Typically, mid-market companies have expectations for results from salespeople within six to twelve months. However, without good training and support, it's often impossible to achieve these timelines. This leads to failure for both the company and the salesperson.

REPORTING
AND METRICS

The next section of lessons focuses on reporting and metrics. There's scant benchmarking and data publicly available to help B2B organizations understand what results they can expect and when. This section will help bridge the gap.

Lesson Sixteen
IT TAKES TIME

The goal of every B2B marketing leader is to build a revenue-generation machine that delivers predictable outcomes based on certain inputs, a machine that enables the revenue generation team to forecast with reasonable certainty what a 10% increase in marketing investment will generate in revenue and profitability, and when.

That's the goal. But every marketing leader I talked with agreed that it takes a lot of time and effort to get there. When I asked each leader how long it had taken for them to achieve this goal in their current company, the majority of them said, "Still working on it!" For the others, their answers ranged between two and three years. So executives working to create marketing that is a finely tuned revenue-generating engine should take heart. Even for the best and most experienced B2B marketers, it's an extended journey.

Because the road is long, marketing leaders have identified some milestones to measure progress along the way. I've synthesized their experience into a framework that can be calibrated to an individual company based on its industry, target market, marketing strategy, and initial level of marketing performance.

Milestones in Building a Revenue-Generation Engine

First 100 Days:

In the first 100 days, marketing leaders have three primary goals. The first is to refine or confirm the marketing strategy, including clarifying the target market and defining the company's value proposition. This is a vital starting point as all the marketing activity flows from the strategy.

The second goal in the first 100 days is to build a marketing foundation, which might include an updated brand identity, overhauling or tweaking the website, or developing new sales collateral that accurately portrays the strategy. Different companies will have different foundation elements, but the benefit of getting a foundation in place in the first 100 days is two-fold. First, some of the foundation will be seen as tangible outputs. While they're not the most important results of marketing (like leads and revenue), they are the first demonstration to the company of what marketing is doing. This is important because people need to see that things are happening in marketing, in relatively short order. The second reason a foundation in the first 100 days is needed is that it supports other activities like raising awareness and generating leads. As Pina Sciarra said, "Without a clear value proposition and a website that accurately portrays the company, the other marketing initiatives and investments will be wasted."

The third goal for the first 100 days is to establish benchmarks for performance. Marketing leaders measure existing marketing performance on a number of different parameters – everything from website traffic to lead generation and conversion rates. Not all of these parameters will ultimately be included in a scorecard, as they won't all be indicators of success, but marketers will start with a long list of parameters and over time will identify which are most closely correlated with success.

Months Four through Twelve:

After the completion of the first 100 days, marketers will get the "marketing machine" rolling. This involves finalizing the foundation (realistically, some companies will not be able to get the strategy and foundation completed in 100 days), beginning to develop and disseminate content, and undertaking lead generation and market awareness activities. The content development process will be established and non-marketing employees will be involved in developing content, which takes some practice. Specific campaigns will be launched and results measured. The company's thought leadership position will begin to be established. Marketers will be able to measure performance through the benchmarks they established in the first 100 days. Results will be achieved in engagement (such as prospects attending a webinar), and leads (both qualified and unqualified) will be generated. By the end of year one, the revenue-generation engine will be built and functioning.

Year Two:

At the end of year one, marketing leaders will analyze their ROI. In many B2B environments, there may not yet be a positive ROI on marketing. The cost of establishing the foundation and getting marketing underway is high, which makes positive ROI hard to achieve in the first twelve months.

Christina DiLallo, when looking at her experience at Newcomp, said, "The impact of marketing was more obvious in year two than in year one – it doubled." That sentiment was echoed across the twenty leaders. The point of doing the ROI analysis at the end of year one is to see where things stand, identify tactics and programs that aren't generating sufficient results, create the plan for year two, and determine where the budget can best be invested.

"The *impact of marketing* was more obvious
in year two than in year one – it doubled."

Over the course of year two, the operations of marketing should become standardized, which makes the team more efficient and able to generate and support more output. That's the point of year two – to fine-tune the marketing machine. With the engine built, the team can accelerate performance. Measurements can be honed in year two – some parameters will highly correlate with qualified lead generation and revenue conversion, others won't. Some programs and initiatives will be effective, some won't – the team will only know through measurement and it will be obvious which programs to de-fund. And lastly, some tweaks to the strategy will be needed in year two – the amount will depend on the speed of evolution of the industry in which the company operates.

Year Three:

By year three, the marketing and sales teams should be well integrated and function as a revenue-generation team. There should be a solid pipeline, and the teams should understand what sources generate what types of leads. The teams should be able to correlate different kinds of marketing tactics with success at various stages of the purchasing process, and continually innovate with messaging and campaigns. They should know the conversion rates for their investments and activities, and forecasting should be reasonably accurate – the organization knows what a dollar spent in a particular tactic will generate in terms of landed business.

By this time, marketing leaders can establish benchmarks for the results they expect based on the data they have. For example, one of the marketing leaders I interviewed expects to generate ten times marketing spend in the pipe and three times spend in qualified leads from every campaign the marketing team undertakes. So every $10 spent on a campaign is expected to generate $100 in the pipe and $30 in qualified leads. It took three years for the marketing leader to determine those benchmarks. But when he did, he knew that the revenue-generation engine had been built and fine-tuned.

> Every $10 spent on a campaign is expected to generate $100 in the pipe and $30 in *qualified leads*. It took three years for the marketing leader to determine those benchmarks.

Calibrating the Framework

For marketers who operate in industries with a slow buying cycle, it may take another year to get to this stage. For those who work in industries with a quick buying cycle, it's possible to get to this stage within two years if there is discipline among the sales and marketing leaders.

Ross Nepean at TAB provided an important tip for B2B marketers about these timelines, and the performance they can expect to see at various stages. Because of the deal sizes in B2B, it's likely that there will be lumpy data. On a quarter-to-quarter basis, some big deals will land, and some won't. It means that a single month, quarter, or year of results can be misleading. So it's important for leaders to look at rolling trends before they make big decisions when evaluating and planning marketing performance.

Lesson Seventeen
SOME IMPORTANT THINGS
ARE HARD TO MEASURE

Einstein said, "Not everything that can be counted counts, and not everything that counts can be counted." This is also true in B2B marketing. Though marketing has made strides over the last decade in improving the tracking and measurement of results, there are still elements that are difficult to measure, especially given the complexity of B2B purchases. But this doesn't make these undertakings any less important.

One of the main issues when it comes to measurement for B2B marketers is that individual campaigns are measurable, but overall marketing is difficult to measure. That's because a single campaign is rarely responsible for generating a qualified B2B lead – there are usually multiple touch points that contribute to a prospect contacting a vendor. While individual leads can be triggered by a single campaign, it is often inaccurate to attribute a lead to just one touch point. B2B buying is more multifaceted than that.

> While individual leads can be triggered by a single campaign, it is often inaccurate to attribute a lead to just one touch point. B2B buying is *move multifaceted* than that.

Non-marketing executives often want to focus on leads as the only metric that matters in marketing. Every CMO I interviewed rejected the concept that lead generation was all that mattered for revenue generation. Here's why:

Revenue generation is a function of all the facets of marketing – strategy, market awareness, lead generation, sales support and retention. Every facet contributes to the success of the others in a linked chain. To focus on just one element is to impair the overall impact and power of marketing.

Some facets of marketing are harder to measure than others. Among them, market awareness is the most complex. To raise awareness is to build a company's reputation in the market so that it's both known and respected by potential customers. Every marketing leader I spoke with talked about the importance of raising market awareness.

The challenge, though, is that quantifying and measuring market awareness is complex and expensive. For consumer companies, like food and entertainment businesses, evaluating market awareness is easier – they have a large target market and can conduct research through tools like online polls. It's a different story in B2B. Companies would need to survey potential buyers rather than the general population. In many cases, it's expensive just to put a list of those people together, let alone try to reach them for a survey. For these reasons, I rarely see B2B companies measuring market awareness. The benefits just don't outweigh the costs.

But even though measuring market awareness is difficult, that doesn't make it any less important for B2B companies. For those who target senior executives, market awareness tactics are often more effective and important than lead generation. Leslie Carter knows that one of her company's key target markets is C-Suite executives of large companies with more than 1,000 employees. These are difficult people to get to. She knows that a lead generation campaign, like calls directly to the CEO or email campaigns, will not be effective. This means using thought leadership (for example, presenting findings from meaningful studies at leadership conferences) will be more effective in getting on the radar of her target market.

Another challenging aspect of measurement for B2B marketers is that marketing is not just about customer acquisition. As Mike Hennessy commented, marketing is about the lifetime value of a customer. The value of lifetime customer relationships should be taken into account when measuring marketing ROI, because the revenue a customer generates in their first year or deal may be just a small fraction of the business it does with a company over its lifetime.

Branding is also difficult to measure. I'm asked from time to time what the ROI of a branding initiative will be. There's no equation for that – a company's brand identity is intrinsic to its reputation and ability to secure revenue. But the brand identity (logo) pales in comparison to

> The value of marketing isn't just about customer acquisition – it's about the *lifetime value* of a customer.

the importance of excellent products, customer service, and innovation. Usually a branding initiative is relevant for a B2B company when its branding doesn't reflect the quality of the business. We've all seen B2B companies whose logos were last updated in the '90s and look like they were drawn by the fourteen-year-old nephew of the CFO. Most B2B companies who need a new corporate identity know they need one.

One last point from the marketing leaders on the challenge of measurement in B2B marketing came from Camille Kennedy. Based on her experience with Hip Digital, Camille believes that determining the right metrics is among the most demanding tasks that B2B marketers face. There are many elements to success. In Camille's case, she advocated for a marketing automation platform which allowed for a more complex lead life cycle model and advanced reporting. The system now automates the scoring of leads and measurement of what's effective. But prior to implementing the system, the process for identifying conversion rates and what was effective among the marketing tools and tactics was *manual*. The process required hard work and discipline; it took several months of collaboration amongst the marketing and sales teams to establish the metrics.

And Camille is hardly alone in this experience; of the twenty marketing leaders, about half indicated they were using or had used a *manual* process on a monthly or quarterly basis to evaluate marketing performance and determine the contribution that marketing was making to revenue. Great B2B marketers don't shy away from this difficult analysis of marketing performance – because they know that to understand what's working, they need the data. And they also know that ultimately, some aspects of marketing are difficult to measure – but that doesn't make them any less important.

> Great B2B marketers don't shy away from doing a *manual calculation* of marketing performance – because they know that to understand what's working, they need the data.

Lesson Eighteen
DON'T REPORT MARKETING METRICS OUTSIDE THE MARKETING TEAM

Though possibly controversial, this is among my favorite lessons from the marketing leaders. The lesson is this: don't share marketing metrics outside of the marketing department.

This sounds counter-intuitive so I'll unpack it a bit. The first element of the lesson is about marketing metrics. Marketers track dozens of metrics to gauge how various campaigns are working. Many of these metrics are granular and don't mean much unless combined with other measurements. Some examples of this are email open rates and click-throughs, the length of time visitors remain on the website, and media mentions. There are literally hundreds of metrics that are reasonable for marketers to track that fall into this category of marketing metrics.

> Marketers track dozens of *metrics* to gauge how programs are working. Many of these metrics don't mean much unless combined with other metrics.

But the problem with these metrics is that when granular marketing metrics are reported outside the marketing department, they can be perceived as being the goal of marketers. For example, if a marketing team shares the email open rate, non-marketing executives might think that the marketers have email open rates as their goal. Of course, smart marketers know that revenue generation is their goal, and that email open rate is just one of the many gauges they look at to get them to their goal.

I've seen many instances of this — even when marketers do a tremendous job of framing marketing metrics in the context of a revenue-generation goal. Somehow, presenting granular marketing data to non-marketers makes them think marketers are focused on the wrong goals.

That's why I like the idea of not sharing marketing metrics outside of the marketing team. It avoids this issue of non-marketing executives getting side-tracked by operational data. If marketers share only the ultimate goals and metrics — typically qualified leads, revenue and profitability — no one will think they have the wrong priorities or don't understand what marketing's real job is.

Keep in mind that just because marketers aren't reporting marketing data outside of the marketing department, that doesn't mean they aren't reporting it *inside* the marketing team. Marketers know that the desired outcome of qualified leads, revenue, and profitability are the sum total of the many marketing activities, initiatives, and investments they undertake — and that they need to measure all of those activities to gauge performance on a frequent basis. So they have a very detailed scorecard *within* the marketing team for evaluating performance. This scorecard will include dozens of metrics (or more) that help them track and refine results. They just don't share it outside of the marketing function.

Andrew Jenkins offered a caveat to this rule, however. In his experience with implementing digital marketing and social media strategies in large companies, he's seen many examples of silo behaviour — where one team doesn't know what the other team is doing, and certainly doesn't understand why they're doing it. He feels that only reporting on marketing outcomes is a dangerous path and that more detailed reporting leads to better cross-functional understanding and collaboration. In the absence of knowledge of what other teams are working on, it's difficult for people to work effectively together. His recommendation is for marketing leaders to take a hybrid approach to reporting — somewhere between the level of granularity that's reported within the marketing team and the scorecard that the Board of Directors would be interested in.

And Susan Smart provided an additional consideration: "The extent of metrics that you share in the organization should correspond to the nature of the organization and the individual you're reporting to. Some organizations are extremely analytical — if that's the case, provide more metrics and data. Other organizations and individuals are more big-picture oriented. They'll want to know the general direction and success, but they won't be interested in the details. When that's the case, don't overdo the scorecard."

The extent of metrics that you share in the organization should correspond to the *nature of the organization* and the individual you're reporting to.

PLANNING FOR LONG-TERM SUCCESS

This last section addresses how to achieve marketing success over the long term. In earlier sections I mentioned the short-term challenges that B2B marketers face, such as the need to deliver quick wins, set reasonable expectations, and allocate resources effectively. Once marketers have been successful in the short term, they can pay attention to shaping the long-term evolution of marketing. That's the focus of the last two lessons:

Lesson Nineteen
TEST AND REFINE, EVOLVE OVER TIME

Good B2B marketing comes from having a clear strategy and using the right tools to translate that strategy into action. Many elements within strategy and tactics change regularly, so a good B2B marketer is always testing and refining, and evolving their plan based on internal and external factors. Here are three reasons to consider changing a marketing strategy.

1. Changes in External Market Conditions

Every market and industry changes over time. Sometimes there are major economic cycle shifts, like the recession of 2008/2009. And more frequently there are changes on a customer or competitor level – new competitors emerge, old competitors are acquired, a large customer's operations move to a different region, new technologies arise that alter the value of a particular solution, a once cutting edge product becomes entirely commoditized. All of these factors impact the success of a given strategy and must be responded to in order to keep a company competitive.

Marketers have to stay informed of market changes and adapt to new conditions in order to keep the company competitive over the long term.

2.   New Company Situation

It's not just external factors that affect a company's strategy. One of the most important elements in setting strategy is the company's own skills, resources, and capabilities – its current situation. Marketing can have a radical impact on these factors. Many B2B marketers have been in situations where the company they're working with started out with no reputation whatsoever, but after a year or two of effective marketing, the company becomes a known entity in the marketplace. That affords new opportunities – a company with a credible reputation can do more to get its message out to a wider audience, engage more deeply with prospects, and bring new innovative products to market quickly. That means the company can put a different marketing strategy in place to leverage and build on its reputation – an option it might not have been able to pursue when it first started marketing.

3.   Changing Tactics and Marketing Capacity

Once a marketing team has established the marketing function, it becomes adept at executing various facets of marketing operations. Because the team has built a marketing machine that works, and the company understands the process and mechanics of developing and distributing content, it's usually able to take on more marketing activities.

Most marketers invest 10% – 15% of their budget per year in trying new tools and tactics to see what results they can achieve.

For example, once the team has done a few white papers, it develops an efficient system of production and distribution, meaning it needs to exert less energy on the process itself and can instead concentrate on the content. That means the team can move onto more complex, higher value marketing activities that it may not have had the capacity to undertake earlier.

At the same time, companies also need to keep up with shifts in communication technology and patterns of communication. Every year there are new communication tools and technologies, and marketers have to balance the use of them in order to stay current, retire old tools that don't work as well as they once did, but also avoid pursuing anything that is "bleeding edge." Most marketers invest 10% – 15% of their budget per year in trying new tools and tactics to see what results they can achieve.

Great B2B marketers are constantly alert to changes in the business environment and new strategic and tactical opportunities.

Lesson Twenty
MARKETERS HAVE TO PAY FOR THEMSELVES

This last lesson comes from Dawn Abankwah. It's here as a summary of the expertise, attitude and outlook of great B2B marketers, and as parting words of wisdom to guide future great B2B marketers. The lesson is about the mindset of B2B marketers.

Dawn has worked in many B2B environments where marketing had a very limited budget, and sometimes no budget at all. That meant Dawn had to find ways to create funds in order to be able to afford any marketing initiatives. For example, when she was running the gift card business at HBC, she identified an opportunity to offer clients a customized service that HBC previously hadn't charged customers for. Because clients valued the customization, they paid for it – which enabled Dawn to generate funds that she could then use for other marketing initiatives. In this way, she generated her own marketing budget. With that money she was able to roll out more initiatives, which in turn generated more funds that could be invested in marketing, and so on.

That's how great B2B marketers think. They combine a healthy dose of business acumen, with personal responsibility, and entrepreneurship.

> Great B2B marketers combine a healthy dose of business acumen, with personal responsibility, and *entrepreneurship*.

It's the dream of B2B company owners to find marketers who think like that – marketers who enter a business, figure out how to create extra profits that can fuel a marketing department, and then grow from there and continually invest in new ways to generate even more profit.

That attitude is incredibly important in B2B. With so many companies new to marketing, mid-market B2Bs need people who can start with a limited budget and make things happen. And it all starts with a marketer's mindset of paying for themselves. It boils down to the concept of ROI, which unfortunately is not always well understood in marketing. The short version of ROI for marketers is that whatever their own salaries, benefits and employment costs are, plus the budget for the marketing activities they want to do, has to be surpassed by the amount of additional profit that their marketing activities generate.

Here's an example. If a marketer's salary is $60,000, their total cost to their employer is about $81,000 (includes employment insurance, employer health tax, workers compensation, benefits, IT, and other administrative costs). Their marketing budget is $50,000. Based on that, the total cost of the marketing department is $131,000. On the revenue side, the company sells services at a 40% gross margin. So for the marketing department to break even, it must generate an additional $327,500 in revenue (40% of $327,500 is $131,000). That's just to break even (100% ROI). For the marketing department to deliver an ROI of 150%, it must generate $500,000 in additional revenues. Most marketers don't think about this math, but they should because it's how business leaders think about the marketing investment they're making. Marketers need to understand the profit margins of the businesses they're working in, and how they're going to generate more profits than they cost.

> For a marketing program to break-even, it needs to *deliver* as much *profit* as it cost. A $100,000 marketing program needs to deliver $100,000 of profit (not just $100,000 of revenue).

The ROI calculation should be one of the guiding principles for how marketers think about their roles and what their mandate is. They still have the challenge of proposing and securing a reasonable budget. And unfortunately, there's relatively little information in the public domain about B2B marketing budgets. But the marketing leaders offered guidance on marketing budgets for new product launches as well as for regular annual marketing activities. A rule of thumb for launching new B2B products is that the marketing budget to support the launch and the first year in market should be equal to 5% of the year five revenue target. So a product that is being launched now with the goal of reaching $5 million in annual revenue by year five should have a $250,000 marketing plan.

For annual marketing budgets, the marketing leaders and my own experience suggest a range of 1% – 4% of target gross revenues. There are industries where that is much higher (software - 15%) and even lower (distributors - 0.5%). Within that range, B2B companies calibrate the right budget based on a number of factors, including:

- the size of the company (larger companies can spend proportionally less on marketing than smaller companies)

- stage of growth (companies at earlier stages of growth will invest a higher proportion in marketing)

- growth ambitions (a company that wants to grow aggressively will invest more than a company that wants to grow modestly)

- geographic scope (companies who pursue global markets have higher marketing spend than those who operate in a tight geographic region)

- maturity of the industry (mature industries typically spend less in marketing)

- chosen strategy (positioning, distribution strategy, and chosen target markets will dictate if a higher marketing spend is needed)

The good news about setting budgets and having a mindset of paying for themselves is that B2B marketers *should* be able to pay for themselves. As Camille Kennedy said, she had a relatively easy time of asking for and receiving additional marketing investment from her company after she had demonstrated that she could make marketing work for the company, and that

THE SEVEN DEADLY
SINS OF MARKETING

Avoid the Seven Sins of Marketing

As a wrap up of the twenty lessons, let's look at what happens when these principles aren't followed. The "Seven Deadly Sins of Marketing" cause millions of wasted marketing dollars every year. To be successful in driving revenues through marketing efforts, don't commit these errors!

The Seven Deadly Sins of Marketing

1. Lacking a Marketing Strategy and Plan

Most businesses and business leaders have a bias towards action. Action is good, but action without direction isn't. Marketing can be fun and exciting – but without a firm grip on the strategy (who's the target market, what's our value proposition, what's our positioning), lots of marketing activities and investment will be wasted.

2. Ignoring Buyer Behavior

Companies often think about products and services from their own viewpoint rather than from the perspective of the buyer. Marketing a product that has better technical specifications than the competitors' is not a guaranteed success. To be truly successful, B2B marketers need to fully and completely understand the buying process — what's important to buyers, how they buy, and who's involved in the purchasing decision. Without this knowledge, it's impossible to develop the right messages and choose the right tactics for successful revenue generation.

3. Prioritizing Sales and Rejecting Marketing

Many B2B companies succeed in their early years by focusing on sales. At the start, it's vital to develop a track record, and direct relationships with pilot customers is the best way to establish one. But investing in sales doesn't accelerate growth the way investing in marketing does — and B2B leaders have to assess when to make the shift from adding salespeople to adding marketing resources.

4. Failing to Integrate Marketing Tactics

There is no silver bullet in marketing. One marketing tactic, used alone, is rarely as effective as when multiple tactics are used together. As the saying goes, the whole is greater than the sum of the parts. While coordinating marketing activities across tactics and channels requires effort, it brings much stronger results.

5. Inconsistency

Often a B2B company will launch a big marketing initiative — a website launch or a trade show appearance — and then stop any marketing efforts within a few months. They get bored, run out of resources to manage the effort, or feel it's not worth the work because they haven't seen immediate results. Or they make individualized, one-off marketing efforts sporadically over the year. This hot and cold approach is a terrible waste of money.

6.   Expecting Instant Results

Today, business moves faster than ever — we get the status of our order in seconds, receive month-end accounting statements in hours, and ship products in days. We want marketing to move just as fast, but relationships cannot develop in an instant and trust must be gained over time. Slow, steady progress is the key to B2B marketing success.

7.   Not Setting Goals

Marketing is a black box for many B2B leaders. They put money in, but aren't sure what comes out or how to find out. Measuring marketing is not always easy, but like any business function, it must be measured. Setting goals and assessing results is the first step.

I hope the twenty lessons serve you well in making marketing work in your organization, whether you're the CEO or the newly minted marketing manager. Please let me know how your efforts are going, and if you have additional lessons to share!

Twitter: @MezzLisa
Email: lisa@theradicalsalesshift.com

Acknowledgements

Without the clients and team at The Mezzanine Group, this book never would have been an idea, let alone a reality. It was their experiences over the last several years that prompted my interest in how the New Buyer was bringing radical changes to the revenue generation efforts of B2B companies. Thanks to each of the fantastic professionals at Mezzanine and all of our great clients for sharing your knowledge and perspectives on the new reality of revenue generation. A special thanks to Jennifer Velagic and Kimberley Wakefield of Mezzanine who worked with me over the last year to bring the book into being.

The twenty marketing leaders were incredibly gracious for sharing their time with me – and even more importantly, for freely offering their expertise. Thanks to each of the twenty leaders for your generosity of spirit. The exceptional B2B marketing leaders of tomorrow will benefit today from your insights, experience and pragmatic advice.

Thanks also to the members of my TAG group, Mezzanine's advisor Steve Hancock, Ted Mercer who provided input on the Sales Diagnostic, and all of the owners and leaders of mid-market B2B companies who have shared their journey and experiences with me.